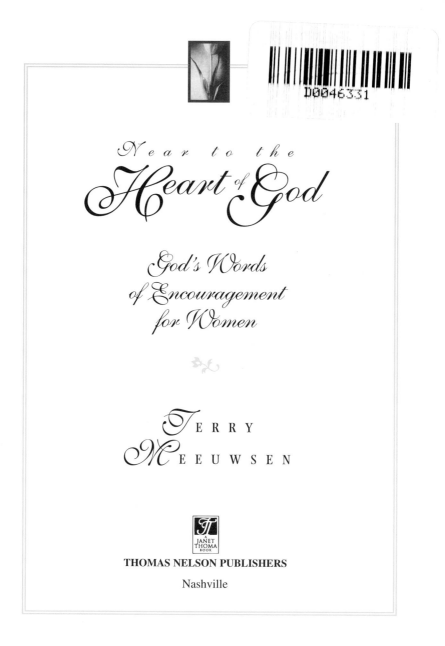

Near to the Heart of God

God's Words of Encouragement for Women

TERRY MEEUWSEN

A JANET THOMA BOOK

THOMAS NELSON PUBLISHERS

Nashville

Published in Nashville, Tennessee, by Thomas Nelson, Inc., Publishers.

Library of Congress Cataloging-in-Publication Data
Meeuwsen, Terry Anne.
    Near to the heart of God / Terry Meeuwsen.
      p.   cm.
    ISBN 0-7852-7060-4 (hc)
    1. Women—Prayer—books and devotions—English.   2. Bible—
Devotional literature.   3. Women—Religious life.   I. Title.
BV4844.M44   1998
242'.643—dc21   97-35181
                                                         CIP

Printed in the United States of America
1 2 3 4 5 6 QPK 03 02 01 00 99 98

To Grandma Hazel, who was a quiet but constant reflection of Jesus. Her legacy of faith and unconditional love made all the difference.

Contents

Part One
The Basis for God's Promises

Part Two
Living the Christian Life

PRAYER

OBEDIENCE

✨

$\mathscr{P}$ a r t $\mathscr{T}$ h r e e
Relationships

Part Four

In Difficult Times

$\mathcal{P}$art $\mathcal{F}$ive
Closing

Acknowledgments

Writing a book is a little like having a baby. When the "baby" is born, there is a time of wonderful celebration. But some pretty intense moments usually precede the birth. Two very special women came alongside me in this process and made all the difference.

Janet Thoma has been a guardian angel for me in the publishing world. Her wisdom, encouragement, and support were invaluable; her friendship, an extra blessing.

Rhonda Palser is my assistant, organizer, watchdog, administrator, and friend extraordinaire. Her creative input is found throughout this book. From the beginning she embraced this project as if it were her own, and I am deeply grateful to her.

I thank my family for their patience and the freedom they gave me to follow God's calling.

Finally, I want to thank the Lord for the powerful, living, life-changing Word of God. "Let the word of Christ dwell in you richly in all wisdom, teaching and admonishing one another in psalms and hymns and spiritual songs, singing with grace in your hearts to the Lord" (Colossians 3:16).

Introduction:
God's Promises

My husband and I are not New Year's Eve revelers, but I do feel a fresh enthusiasm at the thought of starting a brand-new year. If you are like me, you feel a bit breathless as you reflect how quickly the past year flew by. Each New Year's Eve I take the time to sit quietly before the Lord and ask Him what He wants me to focus on in the coming year. Some things are givens, like my relationships with my husband and my children. Being in the Word is another.

This year, however, the Lord was telling me to get into the Word as I'd never been in it before. I felt an urgency and almost a warning in it. God was saying, Do more than just read it. Tuck it away in your heart.

At that time I had no idea I'd be writing this book. As I've shared these stories of God's incredible faithfulness and listed the Scriptures that apply, my heart has rejoiced all over again at the sheer goodness of God and His overwhelming heart for us.

This book is divided into sections, and each section has various topics. If you are struggling with a particular issue, you may want to turn directly to it and find out what the living Word of God has to say. If you happen to be in one of those wonderful refreshing respites in your Christian walk, where the battles are not raging at the moment, you might want to start from the beginning and let God speak to your heart as you go.

It seems that we're all in one of those two places. Paul says we are running a race and encourages us to persevere and endure (see Hebrews 12). To me, it's a lot like a boxing match. Most of the time we're in the heat of battle. Every once in a while we get to sit down, water is poured over us, and we're refreshed. Any wounds we've received are cleaned and treated; our team surrounds us and gives us encouragement and advice. We catch our breath and get refocused. But the purpose is always to get back in the ring and finish the match.

Whether you are in the ring right now or resting on the sidelines, I encourage you to be in the Word. In 2 Timothy 4:2-5 Paul writes,

> Preach the word! Be ready in season and out of season. Convince, rebuke, exhort, with all longsuffering and teaching. For the time will come when they will not endure sound doctrine, but according to their own desires, because they have itching ears, they will heap up for themselves teachers; and they will turn their ears away from the truth, and be turned aside to fables. But you be watchful in all things, endure afflictions, do the work of an evangelist, fulfill your ministry.

I pray that this book will encourage you to press on as you run the race. I'll see you at the finish line.

Jerry Meeuwsen

Part One

❧

*The
Basis for God's
Promises*

"I will never

forget Your precepts,

For by them

You have given

me life."

—Psalm 119:93

Why the Word?

✦

When I first made a commitment to Christ in the early seventies, the Word of God cut through the hardness of my heart and caused me to recognize my need for the Savior. I had been singing professionally and was a self-sufficient, self-centered, cynical young woman. I thought I knew what I wanted and what it would take to make me happy. I had set about trying to achieve those goals with fervor. Spurning God wasn't a conscious effort on my part. He simply wasn't part of the equation.

I grew up in Wisconsin and attended church regularly, knew catechism, could verbalize church doctrine, and was baptized and confirmed. But I had never read the Word of God. I knew nothing about it. In our home we went to church regularly, prayed before meals and at bedtime, and observed Christian holidays. I knew *about* God but I didn't *know* Him.

Many years later when a young girl asked me if I was a Christian, I wasn't sure how to answer. She gave me a little pamphlet called "The Four Spiritual Laws," and that night, alone in my hotel room, I read the biblical plan of salvation. As I read the pamphlet, the Scriptures practically leaped off the page at me. I recognized how far away from God I was. I was also drawn to a sense of purity and righteousness in the Scriptures. I wasn't sure if God was real. But I knew that if what I was reading was available, I needed it. The Word of God convicted me of my sin and at the same time revealed God's love to me.

I'd had preconceived ideas about the Bible even though I'd never read it. I thought it was impossible to understand and that it contradicted itself. Fortunately, the young girl who had given me that little pamphlet also gave me a modern translation of the New Testament. I grudgingly agreed to read a chapter a day. To my amazement, I couldn't put it down. It was all totally new to me.

I didn't know the Old Testament from the New

Testament. I didn't realize that Matthew, Mark, Luke, and John were four accounts of the life of Christ. As I read some of the same gospel accounts I was irritated because I thought someone was moving my book marker. I had no idea that Jesus was coming again. But I began to understand how much God loved me, and I began to walk with Him.

What an incredible journey it's been. Through it all, His Word has been a steady, unfailing compass. God's Word says, "My people are destroyed for lack of knowledge" (Hosea 4:6). Yet God's great love letter to us is at our fingertips. He's given us the instruction manual for all creation, and it's filled with advice, principles, and promises. I encourage you to get into the Word yourself. As you read these jewels of Scripture taken from God's Holy Word, I am praying that your faith will be built and your heart encouraged. May He touch *you* right where you are with His grace and His love.

Father God, thank You for the gift of Your Word. Teach us Your ways and reveal Your heart to us.

The Basis for God's Promises

You search the Scriptures, for in them you think you have eternal life; and these are they which testify of Me.

JOHN 5:39

Therefore whoever hears these sayings of Mine, and does them, I will liken him to a wise man who built his house on the rock: and the rain descended, the floods came, and the winds blew and beat on that house; and it did not fall, for it was founded on the rock.

MATTHEW 7:24–25

Every word of God is pure;
He is a shield to those who put their trust in Him.

PROVERBS 30:5

For the word of God is living and powerful, and sharper than any two-edged sword, piercing even to the division of soul and spirit, and of joints and marrow, and is a discerner of the thoughts and intents of the heart.

HEBREWS 4:12

So now, brethren, I commend you to God and to the word of His grace, which is able to build you up and give you an inheritance among all those who are sanctified.

ACTS 20:32

Heaven and earth will pass away, but My words will by no means pass away.

MARK 13:31

For as the rain comes down, and the snow
   from heaven,
And do not return there,
But water the earth,
And make it bring forth and bud,
That it may give seed to the sower
And bread to the eater,
So shall My word be that goes forth from My
   mouth;
It shall not return to Me void,
But it shall accomplish what I please,
And it shall prosper in the thing for which I
   sent it.

ISAIAH 55:10–11

Blessed be the LORD, who has given rest to His people Israel, according to all that He promised. There has not failed one word of all His good promise, which He promised through His servant Moses.

1 KINGS 8:56

My son, give attention to my words;
Incline your ear to my sayings.
Do not let them depart from your eyes;
Keep them in the midst of your heart;
For they are life to those who find them,
And health to all their flesh.

PROVERBS 4:20–22

The Bible—Our Comfort

For whatever things were written before were written for our learning, that we through the patience and comfort of the Scriptures might have hope.

ROMANS 15:4

This is my comfort in my affliction,
For Your word has given me life.

PSALM 119:50

Unless Your law had been my delight,
I would then have perished in my affliction.

PSALM 119:92

So then faith comes by hearing, and hearing by the
word of God.

ROMANS 10:17

The Bible—Our Guide

This Book of the Law shall not depart from your
mouth, but you shall meditate in it day and night,
that you may observe to do according to all that is
written in it. For then you will make your way
prosperous, and then you will have good success.

JOSHUA 1:8

Then Jesus said to those Jews who believed Him,
"If you abide in My word, you are My disciples
indeed. And you shall know the truth, and the truth
shall make you free."

JOHN 8:31–32

All Scripture is given by inspiration of God, and is
profitable for doctrine, for reproof, for correction, for
instruction in righteousness, that the man of God

may be complete, thoroughly equipped for every
good work.

2 Timothy 3:16–17

*W*hen you roam, they will lead you;
When you sleep, they will keep you;
And when you awake, they will speak with you.
For the commandment is a lamp,
And the law a light;
Reproofs of instruction are the way of life.

Proverbs 6:22–23

*Y*our word is a lamp to my feet
And a light to my path.

Psalm 119:105

*T*rust in the Lord with all your heart,
And lean not on your own understanding;
In all your ways acknowledge Him,
And He shall direct your paths.

Proverbs 3:5–6

*T*he law of the Lord is perfect, converting the soul;
The testimony of the Lord is sure, making wise
    the simple. . . .
More to be desired are they than gold,
Yea, than much fine gold;

Sweeter also than honey and the honeycomb.
Moreover by them Your servant is warned,
And in keeping them there is great reward.

PSALM 19:7, 10–11

*Y*our ears shall hear a word behind you, saying,
"This is the way, walk in it,"
Whenever you turn to the right hand
Or whenever you turn to the left.

ISAIAH 30:21

*H*ow can a young man cleanse his way?
By taking heed according to Your word. . . .
Your word I have hidden in my heart,
That I might not sin against You.

PSALM 119:9, 11

*A*s He spoke by the mouth of His holy prophets,
Who have been since the world began. . . .
To give light to those who sit in darkness and
the shadow of death,
To guide our feet into the way of peace.

LUKE 1:70, 79

*Y*our testimonies also are my delight
And my counselors.

PSALM 119:24

$\mathcal{N}$evertheless I am continually with You;
You hold me by my right hand.
You will guide me with Your counsel,
And afterward receive me to glory.

PSALM 73:23–24

My Journal Page

Date _____

_____

_____

_____

_____

_____

_____

_____

_____

_____

_____

_____

_____

_____

_____

_____

Part Two

❧

*Living
the Christian
Life*

PRAYER

"But you are a chosen generation,
a royal priesthood, a holy nation,
His own special people, that you may
proclaim the praises of Him who
called you out of darkness into
His marvelous light."

—1 Peter 2:9

Forever Family

Never has the family unit been more at risk than it is today. When the family is weakened in any way, all of society is diminished.

One of my favorite Old Testament stories is of Nehemiah and the rebuilding of the wall around Jerusalem. Nehemiah was a man of prayer, and he didn't do anything without talking to God about it. He knew that God is always present, and Nehemiah prayed even while talking to others or taking part in other activities. As individuals and as families we must always ask the Lord for vision and direction before doing anything. James 4:2 says, "You do not have because you do not ask." Through prayer God guides us.

Our particular family is a mini–United Nations. Andy's family are basically Irish and German; mine are Norwegian, Dutch, German, and English. Our oldest two children are Heinz 57 variety. J. P. is the only pure-blooded one among us. He is Korean. Tyler is biracial and has an African-American and, I think, English heritage.

I pray with my children each night before they go to sleep and ask God to give them vision for who they are in Him. I pray that their identity will not come from their origin of birth or from Andy and me but from their spiritual heritage in the Lord.

Psalm 139:15–16 says, "My frame was not hidden from You, /When I was made in secret, /And skillfully wrought in the lowest parts of the earth. /Your eyes saw my substance, being yet unformed. /And in Your book they all were written, /The days fashioned for me, /When as yet there were none of them."

The way we are conceived, the way we're made, the families we belong to—none of this is accidental. God always knew it would be that way.

Unity is so important in a family, whether it's our own family or the family of God. We need to be a team where *all* the players are important. Nehemiah knew that. The wall around Jerusalem had been destroyed for more than a hundred years. It was so daunting a task that no one before Nehemiah had even attempted to rebuild it. Nehemiah knew it would take the effort of all the citizens of Jerusalem to rebuild that wall. It is likewise true that for our families and the church to live in harmony and be effective, all members need to do their part.

Before one stone was moved on that wall around Jerusalem, the enemy began ridiculing and threatening the people. But the work began. Bit by bit, stone by stone, family by family, that wall began to go up.

Every family was responsible for the part of the wall behind their respective house. As that wall went up, the enemies got angrier. They plotted to lead an army against the city. The people of the city were afraid. They also were tired, for they worked hard. What did Nehemiah do? "We made our prayer to our God, and because of them we set a watch against them day and night" (Nehemiah 4:9).

First, he prayed; second, he acted. The people developed

a plan to protect themselves. Half the men worked while the other half stood guard behind them. They worked from sunrise to sunset and carried their weapons with them at all times. As leaders in our families, we learn a great lesson from Nehemiah. Prayer and action go hand in hand.

Even as those families were responsible for their part of the wall, so *we* are responsible for raising up a godly standard in our own homes. There are many ways of doing that—having devotions, praying for and with one another, giving blessings, recounting God's goodness.

We have worked hard at establishing traditions of togetherness with our children. I lay hands on each one and give them a blessing before they leave for school in the morning. We cook together and have family night as often as possible. We play games together, read together, and pray for one another's needs. Right now they know I need prayer for this book, and they also know that I am praying for their spelling exams, speech meets, and basketball games.

As often as possible, I verbalize how important and

special they are to me. Every night I pray with each child as he or she snuggles into bed. When J. P. was very small I used to say fairly regularly, "Lord, thank You for J. P. He is such a treasure to me." One night, I was tired and shortened my prayer. I felt a tug on my sleeve. "You forgot something, Mama." Those serious little eyes stared piercingly into my own. "I'm your treasure, right?" I held him tightly. "Oh, J. P., you are my treasure. We are family. Never forget it!"

And so it is for us, dear ones. We are the sons and daughters of the living God, His handiwork, created in His image and likeness, the ones for whom He paid a great price. We are His treasure. We are family. Never forget it!

Lord, thank You for making us a part of Your family. Give us wisdom as we establish our own families. When we're tired or afraid, remind us that You specialize in the impossible. Call us to prayer and action. Make us a forever family.

In Prayer

Likewise the Spirit also helps in our weaknesses. For we do not know what we should pray for as we ought, but the Spirit Himself makes intercession for us with groanings which cannot be uttered.

ROMANS 8:26

Call to Me, and I will answer you, and show you great and mighty things, which you do not know.

JEREMIAH 33:3

Then He spoke a parable to them, that men always ought to pray and not lose heart.

LUKE 18:1

Again I say to you that if two of you agree on earth concerning anything that they ask, it will be done for them by My Father in heaven. For where two or three are gathered together in My name, I am there in the midst of them.

MATTHEW 18:19–20

But you, when you pray, go into your room, and when you have shut your door, pray to your Father who is in the secret place; and your Father who sees in secret will reward you openly.

MATTHEW 6:6

Therefore I say to you, whatever things you ask when you pray, believe that you receive them, and you will have them.

MARK 11:24

The LORD is near to all who call upon Him,
To all who call upon Him in truth.
He will fulfill the desire of those who fear Him;
He also will hear their cry and save them.

PSALM 145:18–19

Delight yourself also in the LORD,
And He shall give you the desires of your heart.

PSALM 37:4

The LORD is far from the wicked,
But He hears the prayer of the righteous.

PROVERBS 15:29

Seeing then that we have a great High Priest who has passed through the heavens, Jesus the Son of God, let us hold fast our confession. For we do not have a High Priest who cannot sympathize with our weaknesses, but was in all points tempted as we are, yet without sin. Let us therefore come boldly to the throne of grace, that we may obtain mercy and find grace to help in time of need.

HEBREWS 4:14–16

He shall pray to God, and He will delight in him,
He shall see His face with joy,
For He restores to man His righteousness.

JOB 33:26

For what great nation is there that has God so near to it, as the LORD our God is to us, for whatever reason we may call upon Him?

DEUTERONOMY 4:7

In the day of my trouble I will call upon You,
For You will answer me.

PSALM 86:7

Draw near to God and He will draw near to you. Cleanse your hands, you sinners; and purify your hearts, you double-minded.

JAMES 4:8

Evening and morning and at noon
I will pray, and cry aloud,
And He shall hear my voice.

PSALM 55:17

Pray without ceasing, in everything give thanks;
for this is the will of God in Christ Jesus for you.

1 THESSALONIANS 5:17–18

In Answered Prayer

And whatever you ask in My name, that I will do,
that the Father may be glorified in the Son. If you
ask anything in My name, I will do it.

JOHN 14:13–14

And whatever we ask we receive from Him,
because we keep His commandments and do those
things that are pleasing in His sight.

1 JOHN 3:22

And whatever things you ask in prayer, believing,
you will receive.

MATTHEW 21:22

If you abide in Me, and My words abide in you, you will ask what you desire, and it shall be done for you.

JOHN 15:7

And the prayer of faith will save the sick, and the Lord will raise him up. And if he has committed sins, he will be forgiven. Confess your trespasses to one another, and pray for one another, that you may be healed. The effective, fervent prayer of a righteous man avails much.

JAMES 5:15–16

And in that day you will ask Me nothing. Most assuredly, I say to you, whatever you ask the Father in My name He will give you. Until now you have asked nothing in My name. Ask, and you will receive, that your joy may be full.

JOHN 16:23–24

Now this is the confidence that we have in Him, that if we ask anything according to His will, He hears us. And if we know that He hears us, whatever we ask, we know that we have the petitions that we have asked of Him. If anyone sees his brother sinning a sin which does not lead to death, he will ask, and He will give him life for those who commit sin not leading to death. There is sin leading to death. I do not say that he should pray about that.

1 John 5:14–16

I will bring the one-third through the fire,
Will refine them as silver is refined,
And test them as gold is tested.
They will call on My name,
And I will answer them.
I will say, "This is My people";
And each one will say, "The Lord is my God."

Zechariah 13:9

But know that the Lord has set apart for Himself
    him who is godly;
The Lord will hear when I call to Him.

Psalm 4:3

The eyes of the Lord are on the righteous,
And His ears are open to their cry. . . .
The righteous cry out, and the Lord hears,
And delivers them out of all their troubles.

Psalm 34:15, 17

The LORD is far from the wicked,
But He hears the prayer of the righteous.

PROVERBS 15:29

He shall call upon Me, and I will answer him;
I will be with him in trouble;
I will deliver him and honor him.

PSALM 91:15

It shall come to pass
That before they call, I will answer;
And while they are still speaking, I will hear.

ISAIAH 65:24

O You who hear prayer,
To You all flesh will come.

PSALM 65:2

Then you will call upon Me and go and pray to
Me, and I will listen to you.

JEREMIAH 29:12

Ask, and it will be given to you; seek, and you
will find; knock, and it will be opened to you. For
everyone who asks receives, and he who seeks finds,
and to him who knocks it will be opened.

MATTHEW 7:7–8

If you then, being evil, know how to give good gifts to your children, how much more will your Father who is in heaven give good things to those who ask Him!

MATTHEW 7:11

I will call upon the LORD, who is worthy to
be praised;
So shall I be saved from my enemies.

PSALM 18:3

Call to Me, and I will answer you, and show you great and mighty things, which you do not know.

JEREMIAH 33:3

My Journal Page

Date _____

_____

_____

_____

_____

_____

_____

_____

_____

_____

_____

_____

_____

_____

_____

_____

_____

_____

_____

OBEDIENCE

"Blessed is she who believed,

for there will be a fulfillment

of those things which were told

her from the Lord."

—Luke 1:45

Keep My Commandments

When they were quite young, my two oldest children attended a neighborhood Good News Club. They memorized Bible verses, listened to Bible stories, and sang many songs about the Lord and biblical truths. One of those songs was about obedience. The last line was, "Obedience is the very best way to show that you believe."

It's so easy to "talk the talk," isn't it? But "*walking* the talk" is where the struggle occurs. The Word is clear about this. If we want God to get serious about our concerns, we need to get serious about His. Jesus asked, "Why do you call Me 'Lord, Lord,' and not do the things which I say?" (Luke 6:46). Why do we have such a difficult time with obedience? This struggle goes all the way back to the Garden of Eden.

My little J. P., who is ten years old and struggling with the thought of dying, blurted out one day, "I hate that Adam and Eve. If it hadn't been for them, we'd have been in great shape." The Bible says that from Adam and Eve on down, "all have sinned and fall short of the glory of God" (Romans 3:23). If God's glory is the standard that we compare our sinfulness to, maybe we've been too familiar with God.

When in Israel recently, I asked our guide, Ami Weiss, if Jews in Israel call the prayer cap a *yarmulke* or if they have a Hebrew name for it. He said the cap is called a *kepa*. I asked what that meant. He thought for several minutes, struggling with how to say in English what he thoroughly understood in Hebrew. "It means, 'Know to whom you are speaking.'" Indeed! We are able to commune with the One who created everything that is. John's Gospel tells us that without Him, nothing was made that has been made.

When I invited Christ into my heart and gave Him what was left of my life, I was convicted of my sin by the power of the Word of God. Pastor, author, and teacher Jack Taylor says in *The Word of God with Power*, "He [God] spoke a Book, and lives in His spoken words, constantly speaking His words and causing the power of them to persist across the years." The Word of God is alive and well and full of power. God is still speaking to His people today through *logos* (the written word) and *rhema* (the spoken word). He is looking for those whose hearts are fully committed to Him, those who are willing to be obedient (see 2 Chronicles 16:9).

And what should our response to His Word be? Jack Taylor suggests we look to Mary as an exemplary model. She *learned to listen*, she *heard the Word*, she *received* it, she *confessed* it, she *obeyed* it, she *acted* on it. He writes, "As we hear the Word, and receive it with confession, we get pregnant by the Word of God, pregnant with whatever the Word promises."

Lord, when I hear Your Word, help me to receive it with Mary's gentle faith. Give me the courage to confess it, and the strength to obey it. May it be done to me according to Your Word.

In Obedience

He who has My commandments and keeps them, it is he who loves Me. And he who loves Me will be loved by My Father, and I will love him and manifest Myself to him.

JOHN 14:21

Now by this we know that we know Him, if we keep His commandments. He who says, "I know Him," and does not keep His commandments, is a liar, and the truth is not in him. But whoever keeps His word, truly the love of God is perfected in him. By this we know that we are in Him. He who says he abides in Him ought himself also to walk just as He walked.

1 JOHN 2:3–6

Behold, I set before you today a blessing and a curse: the blessing, if you obey the commandments of the LORD your God which I command you today; and the curse, if you do not obey the commandments of the LORD your God, but turn aside from the way which I command you today, to go after other gods which you have not known.

DEUTERONOMY 11:26–28

$\mathcal{W}$hoever therefore breaks one of the least of these commandments, and teaches men so, shall be called least in the kingdom of heaven; but whoever does and teaches them, he shall be called great in the kingdom of heaven.

MATTHEW 5:19

$\mathcal{I}$f you keep My commandments, you will abide in My love, just as I have kept My Father's commandments and abide in His love.

JOHN 15:10

$\mathcal{T}$herefore keep the words of this covenant, and do them, that you may prosper in all that you do.

DEUTERONOMY 29:9

$\mathcal{F}$or whoever does the will of My Father in heaven is My brother and sister and mother.

MATTHEW 12:50

$\mathcal{O}$h, that they had such a heart in them that they would fear Me and always keep all My commandments, that it might be well with them and with their children forever!

DEUTERONOMY 5:29

If you fear the LORD and serve Him and obey His voice, and do not rebel against the commandment of the LORD, then both you and the king who reigns over you will continue following the LORD your God.

1 SAMUEL 12:14

Not everyone who says to Me, "Lord, Lord," shall enter the kingdom of heaven, but he who does the will of My Father in heaven.

MATTHEW 7:21

So you shall observe My statutes and keep My judgments, and perform them; and you will dwell in the land in safety. Then the land will yield its fruit, and you will eat your fill, and dwell there in safety.

LEVITICUS 25:18–19

But he who looks into the perfect law of liberty and continues in it, and is not a forgetful hearer but a doer of the work, this one will be blessed in what he does.

JAMES 1:25

He who keeps the commandment keeps his soul,
But he who is careless of his ways will die.

PROVERBS 19:16

Now therefore, if you will indeed obey My voice
and keep My covenant, then you shall be a special
treasure to Me above all people; for all the earth is
Mine.

EXODUS 19:5

Blessed are the undefiled in the way,
Who walk in the law of the LORD!
Blessed are those who keep His testimonies,
Who seek Him with the whole heart!

PSALM 119:1–2

If you are willing and obedient,
You shall eat the good of the land.

ISAIAH 1:19

And keep the charge of the LORD your God: to
walk in His ways, to keep His statutes, His
commandments, His judgments, and His
testimonies, as it is written in the Law of Moses, that
you may prosper in all that you do and wherever
you turn.

1 KINGS 2:3

And the world is passing away, and the lust of it; but he who does the will of God abides forever.

1 JOHN 2:17

If you know these things, blessed are you if you do them.

JOHN 13:17

My Journal Page

Date _____

_____

_____

_____

_____

_____

_____

_____

_____

_____

_____

_____

_____

_____

_____

_____

_____

_____

TEMPTATION AND GUILT

"But we have this treasure

in earthen vessels,

that the excellence of the power

may be of God and not of us."

—2 Corinthians 4:7

Treasure in Jars of Clay

Our household is a little wild and woolly. One minute my children are playing nicely together, and the next minute they're waging war. The most frustrating part of parenting, for me, is the never-ending bickering and fighting that go on among siblings. It seems almost impossible for my kids to spend any significant amount of time together without fighting or deliberately irritating one another. (Sounds a lot like the church, doesn't it?!)

I see so much of my own struggle with willfulness reflected in my children. I am always so sorry, after the fact, and yet I may find myself confessing the same sin over again in less than twenty-four hours. If I'm really repentant, how can that be? Paul states it perfectly, "For what I am doing, I do not understand. For what I will to do, that I do not practice; but what I hate, that I do" (Romans 7:15). Getting a spiritual understanding of our dilemma is crucial to overcoming temptation and guilt.

The Bible says, "Your adversary the devil walks about like a roaring lion, seeking whom he may devour" (1 Peter 5:8). It also says, "For we do not wrestle against flesh and blood, but against principalities, against powers, against the rulers of the darkness of this age, against spiritual hosts of wickedness in the heavenly places" (Ephesians 6:12).

We are in a battle that has eternal significance. On the surface it may seem like a personal struggle with some mental or physical area of weakness. That's what Satan would love for you to think. This is *your* problem, *your* weakness, *your* failure. And it's bigger than you are. How he loves to see us defeated in these areas of our lives.

For years I tried to battle these areas of temptation in my life by drumming up willpower, gritting my teeth, and digging in my heels. Once in a while I'd have a victory, but more often than not I'd end up on my face, riddled with guilt before the Lord. Have you ever seen a cat toy with a mouse before finishing it off? The cat will sometimes sit in condescending amusement watching its prey struggling to escape. That's how I felt Satan toyed with me as I struggled to overcome. Then I'd fail and think to myself, *How can I be so weak? I know the Lord; I love the Lord; I know what is right, and I want to change. What's wrong with me?*

If you are in such a struggle about anything, begin reading at verse 7 in chapter 7 of the book of Romans. As you read on into chapter 8 of Romans, you'll come to an incredible solution: "For those who live according to the flesh set their minds on the things of the flesh, but those who live according to the Spirit, the things of the Spirit" (8:5). How do we live in accordance with the Spirit? "For you did not receive the spirit of bondage again to fear, but you received the Spirit of adoption by whom we cry out, 'Abba, Father'" (8:15). The word *abba* actually translates to "daddy."

This, dear friends, is the key to overcoming. When you are in the throes of temptation, run to the Father! Get into

His presence and tap into His power. The Bible tells us that in our weakness God is strong. His presence puts our problems in perspective and floods us with a sense of protection, peace, and power.

If you find yourself in a situation where you've been defeated and are filled with guilt, remember, "There is therefore now no condemnation to those who are in Christ Jesus" (Romans 8:1). Don't let the enemy rub your face in the dirt. God's forgiveness is *always* extended to us. The Bible says that *nothing* can separate us from the love of God. When you are in trouble, run to the heart of the Father.

Abba, Father! Help me! The storm is threatening to overwhelm me, and I am weak. I confess my sins and I ask for Your forgiveness. Fill me with Your Spirit and teach me Your ways. Give me the mind of Christ and a vision for who I am in You. I stand on Your Word, which says that "we are more than conquerors through Him who loved us." I rest in You, my Father.

For Times of Temptation

O wretched man that I am! Who will deliver me from this body of death? I thank God—through Jesus Christ our Lord! So then, with the mind I myself serve the law of God, but with the flesh the law of sin.

ROMANS 7:24–25

No temptation has overtaken you except such as is common to man; but God is faithful, who will not allow you to be tempted beyond what you are able, but with the temptation will also make the way of escape, that you may be able to bear it.

1 CORINTHIANS 10:13

I say then: Walk in the Spirit, and you shall not fulfill the lust of the flesh.

GALATIANS 5:16

For in that He Himself has suffered, being tempted, He is able to aid those who are tempted.

HEBREWS 2:18

*Y*ou are of God, little children, and have overcome them, because He who is in you is greater than he who is in the world.

1 JOHN 4:4

*K*nowing this, that our old man was crucified with Him, that the body of sin might be done away with, that we should no longer be slaves of sin.

ROMANS 6:6

*Y*et in all these things we are more than conquerors through Him who loved us.

ROMANS 8:37

*T*hese things I have spoken to you, that in Me you may have peace. In the world you will have tribulation; but be of good cheer, I have overcome the world.

JOHN 16:33

*F*inally, my brethren, be strong in the Lord and in the power of His might. Put on the whole armor of God, that you may be able to stand against the wiles of the devil. . . . Above all, taking the shield of faith with which you will be able to quench all the fiery darts of the wicked one.

EPHESIANS 6:10–11, 16

$\mathcal{W}$ho gave Himself for our sins, that He might deliver us from this present evil age, according to the will of our God and Father.

Galatians 1:4

$\mathcal{B}$lessed is the man who endures temptation; for when he has been approved, he will receive the crown of life which the Lord has promised to those who love Him. Let no one say when he is tempted, "I am tempted by God"; for God cannot be tempted by evil, nor does He Himself tempt anyone. But each one is tempted when he is drawn away by his own desires and enticed.

James 1:12–14

$\mathcal{A}$nd the Lord said, "Simon, Simon! Indeed, Satan has asked for you, that he may sift you as wheat. But I have prayed for you, that your faith should not fail; and when you have returned to Me, strengthen your brethren.

Luke 22:31–32

$\mathcal{B}$e sober, be vigilant; because your adversary the devil walks about like a roaring lion, seeking whom he may devour. Resist him, steadfast in the faith, knowing that the same sufferings are experienced by your brotherhood in the world.

1 PETER 5:8–9

I do not pray that You should take them out of the world, but that You should keep them from the evil one.

JOHN 17:15

And the God of peace will crush Satan under your feet shortly. The grace of our Lord Jesus Christ be with you. Amen.

ROMANS 16:20

For Times of Guilt

For if our heart condemns us, God is greater than our heart, and knows all things.

1 JOHN 3:20

If we confess our sins, He is faithful and just to forgive us our sins and to cleanse us from all unrighteousness.

1 JOHN 1:9

There is therefore now no condemnation to those who are in Christ Jesus, who do not walk according to the flesh, but according to the Spirit.

ROMANS 8:1

For God did not send His Son into the world to condemn the world, but that the world through Him might be saved. He who believes in Him is not condemned; but he who does not believe is condemned already, because he has not believed in the name of the only begotten Son of God.

JOHN 3:17–18

He will not always strive with us,
Nor will He keep His anger forever.
He has not dealt with us according to our sins,
Nor punished us according to our iniquities.
For as the heavens are high above the earth,
So great is His mercy toward those who fear Him;
As far as the east is from the west,
So far has He removed our transgressions
   from us.

PSALM 103:9–12

For I will be merciful to their unrighteousness, and their sins and their lawless deeds I will remember no more.

HEBREWS 8:12

I will cleanse them from all their iniquity by which they have sinned against Me, and I will pardon all their iniquities by which they have sinned and by which they have transgressed against Me.

JEREMIAH 33:8

For if you return to the LORD, your brethren and your children will be treated with compassion by those who lead them captive, so that they may come back to this land; for the LORD your God is gracious and merciful, and will not turn His face from you if you return to Him.

2 CHRONICLES 30:9

No more shall every man teach his neighbor, and every man his brother, saying, "Know the LORD," for they all shall know Me, from the least of them to the greatest of them, says the LORD. For I will forgive their iniquity, and their sin I will remember no more.

JEREMIAH 31:34

Let us draw near with a true heart in full assurance of faith, having our hearts sprinkled from an evil conscience and our bodies washed with pure water.

HEBREWS 10:22

Let the wicked forsake his way,
And the unrighteous man his thoughts;
Let him return to the LORD,
And He will have mercy on him;
And to our God,
For He will abundantly pardon.

ISAIAH 55:7

Therefore, if anyone is in Christ, he is a new creation; old things have passed away; behold, all things have become new.

2 CORINTHIANS 5:17

Blessed is he whose transgression is forgiven,
Whose sin is covered.

PSALM 32:1

I acknowledged my sin to You,
And my iniquity I have not hidden.
I said, "I will confess my transgressions to the LORD,"
And You forgave the iniquity of my sin. Selah

PSALM 32:5

I, even I, am He who blots out your transgressions
   for My own sake;
And I will not remember your sins.

ISAIAH 43:25

"Therefore I say to you, her sins, which are many,
are forgiven, for she loved much. But to whom little
is forgiven, the same loves little." Then He said to
her, "Your sins are forgiven."

LUKE 7:47–48

Then He said to the woman, "Your faith has saved
you. Go in peace."

LUKE 7:50

Who is a God like You,
Pardoning iniquity
And passing over the transgression of the
   remnant of His heritage?
He does not retain His anger forever,
Because He delights in mercy.
He will again have compassion on us,
And will subdue our iniquities.
You will cast all our sins
Into the depths of the sea.

MICAH 7:18–19

Then He adds, "Their sins and their lawless deeds I will remember no more."

HEBREWS 10:17

I have blotted out, like a thick cloud,
   your transgressions,
And like a cloud, your sins.
Return to Me, for I have redeemed you.

ISAIAH 44:22

In Victory over Sin

Then the Lord knows how to deliver the godly out of temptations and to reserve the unjust under punishment for the day of judgment.

2 PETER 2:9

For sin shall not have dominion over you, for you are not under law but under grace.

ROMANS 6:14

God is faithful, who will not allow you to be tempted beyond what you are able, but with the temptation will also make the way of escape, that you may be able to bear it.

1 CORINTHIANS 10:13

*Y*ou are of God, little children, and have overcome them, because He who is in you is greater than he who is in the world.

1 JOHN 4:4

*Y*our word I have hidden in my heart,
That I might not sin against You.

PSALM 119:11

*H*e who covers his sins will not prosper,
But whoever confesses and forsakes them will
   have mercy.

PROVERBS 28:13

*I*f we confess our sins, He is faithful and just to forgive us our sins and to cleanse us from all unrighteousness.

1 JOHN 1:9

*S*eeing then that we have a great High Priest who has passed through the heavens, Jesus the Son of God, let us hold fast our confession. For we do not have a High Priest who cannot sympathize with our weaknesses, but was in all points tempted as we are, yet without sin. Let us therefore come boldly to the throne of grace, that we may obtain mercy and find grace to help in time of need.

HEBREWS 4:14–16

*I*n this you greatly rejoice, though now for a little while, if need be, you have been grieved by various trials, that the genuineness of your faith, being much more precious than gold that perishes, thought is tested by fire, may be found to praise, honor, and glory at the revelation of Jesus Christ.

1 PETER 1:6–7

*I*t is good that you grasp this,
And also not remove your hand from the other;
For he who fears God will escape them all.

ECCLESIASTES 7:18

*F*or the law of the Spirit of life in Christ Jesus has made me free from the law of sin and death. For what the law could not do in that it was weak through the flesh, God did by sending His own Son in the likeness of sinful flesh, on account of sin: He condemned sin in the flesh, that the righteous requirement of the law might be fulfilled in us who do not walk according to the flesh but according to the Spirit.

ROMANS 8:2–4

From Backsliding

For he who lacks these things is shortsighted, even to blindness, and has forgotten that he was cleansed from his old sins. Therefore, brethren, be even more diligent to make your call and election sure, for if you do these things you will never stumble.

2 PETER 1:9–10

Therefore submit to God. Resist the devil and he will flee from you. Draw near to God and He will draw near to you. Cleanse your hands, you sinners; and purify your hearts, you double-minded. Lament and mourn and weep! Let your laughter be turned to mourning and your joy to gloom. Humble yourselves in the sight of the Lord, and He will lift you up.

JAMES 4:7–10

Do not boast about tomorrow,
For you do not know what a day may bring forth.

PROVERBS 27:1

O wretched man that I am! Who will deliver me from this body of death? I thank God—through Jesus Christ our Lord! So then, with the mind I myself serve the law of God, but with the flesh the law of sin.

ROMANS 7:24–25

He who covers his sins will not prosper,
But whoever confesses and forsakes them will
   have mercy.

PROVERBS 28:13

Being confident of this very thing, that He who has begun a good work in you will complete it until the day of Jesus Christ.

PHILIPPIANS 1:6

Therefore, brethren, be even more diligent to make your call and election sure, for if you do these things you will never stumble.

2 PETER 1:10

The backslider in heart will be filled with his
   own ways,
But a good man will be satisfied from above.

PROVERBS 14:14

I will heal their backsliding,
I will love them freely,
For My anger has turned away from him.

HOSEA 14:4

My Journal Page

Date _____

_____

_____

_____

_____

_____

_____

_____

_____

_____

_____

_____

_____

_____

_____

_____

_____

_____

FORGIVENESS

"*Forgiveness is*

the fragrance a flower leaves

on the heel of the one

who has crushed it."

—Unknown

Happily Ever After

Hopes and dreams are part of all of us. They push us to heights of greatness and often sustain us in unbearable circumstances. As we move toward adulthood, the *hope* of meeting that special someone and the *dream* of a happily-ever-after marriage are alive in most young hearts.

I was twenty-three years old and in the middle of my reign as Miss America when Tom Camburn asked me to marry him. After years of singing professionally and living out of a suitcase, this well-established businessman, who was thirteen years older than I, brought a sense of stability and protection into my life. As a relatively new Christian, I loved the Lord and knew it was important to marry someone who would share my faith. Tom announced one day that he had privately invited Christ into his life. I was thrilled and ignored the fact that I saw no real evidence of any meaningful spiritual growth. I was head over heels in

love, and instead of asking if this was God's plan for my life,
I made my own decision and then asked God to bless it.
That proved to be one of the costliest, most painful mistakes
of my life.

Two years into the marriage, I realized my husband had
a serious drinking problem. But I believed, with the tenacity
of a bulldog, that if I prayed hard enough, was home every
night, cooked well, and just believed for the best, it would
all work out. After all, Christians don't get divorced.

Five years into the marriage, I was left dazed,
disillusioned, confused, rejected, and alone. What do you do
when the dream dies? How do you go on when you've given
your very best and it just isn't good enough? I cried out of
desperation, "God, in the Old Testament You changed the
hearts of kings. Would one little man in Mequon,
Wisconsin, have been so difficult? What will people who
know I'm a Christian think of me?" In the quiet of my heart
I heard the still, small voice say, *Leave your reputation with
Me! I know where you've been; I've seen your tears. Now give Me*

your pain. I was learning about the unconditional love of God, and in time I learned to forgive myself.

Many years after the divorce, when Tom was dying of cancer, I felt the urging of the Lord to call him and reassure him that I had forgiven him and forgotten the hurt in our relationship. "But Lord, he's not *asking* for forgiveness." I felt presumptuous. The Scripture came to me, "Freely you have received, freely give" (Matthew 10:8).

When I obeyed the Lord's urging and talked to Tom, I could hear the relief and release in Tom's voice. In that act of obedience, God healed something in me. A week later Tom died.

Our forgiving others allows *us* to freely receive God's love and His healing in the deep places in our hearts. I'll never know what transpired between Tom and the Lord in the last hours of his life. But just as God's unconditional acceptance of me allowed me to forgive myself and move on, I believe that my extending forgiveness to Tom allowed him to forgive himself and open his heart to God's pure and unconditional love for him. God's ways are so much better than our own.

🌿

Lord, it's hard for me to understand Your unconditional love for me when I seem so unlovable. Thank You for seeing the promise in me instead of the failures. As I receive Your forgiveness, give me a heart that is willing to extend forgiveness out of obedience and gratitude to You—and not because I feel like it or because someone is asking for it.

In Forgiving Others

And whenever you stand praying, if you have anything against anyone, forgive him, that your Father in heaven may also forgive you your trespasses.

MARK 11:25

Then Peter came to Him and said, "Lord, how often shall my brother sin against me, and I forgive him? Up to seven times?" Jesus said to him, "I do not say to you, up to seven times, but up to seventy times seven."

MATTHEW 18:21–22

Bearing with one another, and forgiving one another, if anyone has a complaint against another; even as Christ forgave you, so you also must do.

COLOSSIANS 3:13

For if you forgive men their trespasses, your heavenly Father will also forgive you. But if you do not forgive men their trespasses, neither will your Father forgive your trespasses.

MATTHEW 6:14–15

Therefore
"If your enemy is hungry, feed him;
If he is thirsty, give him a drink;
For in so doing you will heap coals of fire on
   his head."
Do not be overcome by evil, but overcome evil with
good.

ROMANS 12:20–21

But I say to you, love your enemies, bless those
who curse you, do good to those who hate you, and
pray for those who spitefully use you and persecute
you, that you may be sons of your Father in heaven;
for He makes His sun rise on the evil and on the
good, and sends rain on the just and on the unjust.

MATTHEW 5:44–45

For this is commendable, if because of conscience
toward God one endures grief, suffering wrongfully.
For what credit is it if, when you are beaten for
your faults, you take it patiently? But when you
do good and suffer, if you take it patiently, this
is commendable before God. For to this you
were called, because Christ also suffered for us,
leaving us an example, that you should follow His
steps:

"Who committed no sin,
Nor was deceit found in His mouth";
who, when He was reviled, did not revile in return;
when He suffered, He did not threaten, but
committed Himself to Him who judges righteously.

1 PETER 2:19–23

$\mathcal{D}$o not say, "I will recompense evil";
Wait for the LORD, and He will save you.

PROVERBS 20:22

$\mathcal{B}$ut love your enemies, do good, and lend, hoping
for nothing in return; and your reward will be great,
and you will be sons of the Most High. For He is
kind to the unthankful and evil. . . . Judge not, and
you shall not be judged. Condemn not, and you
shall not be condemned. Forgive, and you will be
forgiven.

LUKE 6:35, 37

$\mathcal{B}$lessed are those who are persecuted for
    righteousness' sake,
For theirs is the kingdom of heaven.
Blessed are you when they revile and persecute you,
and say all kinds of evil against you falsely for My
sake. Rejoice and be exceedingly glad, for great is

your reward in heaven, for so they persecuted the prophets who were before you.

MATTHEW 5:10–12

For we know Him who said, "Vengeance is Mine, I will repay," says the Lord. And again, "The LORD will judge His people."

HEBREWS 10:30

Let all bitterness, wrath, anger, clamor, and evil speaking be put away from you, with all malice. And be kind to one another, tenderhearted, forgiving one another, even as God in Christ forgave you.

EPHESIANS 4:31–32

If you are reproached for the name of Christ, blessed are you, for the Spirit of glory and of God rests upon you. On their part He is blasphemed, but on your part He is glorified.

1 PETER 4:14

My Journal Page

Date _____

_____
_____
_____
_____
_____
_____
_____
_____
_____
_____
_____
_____
_____
_____
_____
_____
_____
_____

PERSEVERANCE

"He gives power to the weak,
And to those who have no might
He increases strength.
Even the youths shall faint and be weary,
And the young men shall utterly fall,
But those who wait on the LORD
Shall renew their strength;
They shall mount up with wings like eagles,
They shall run and not be weary,
They shall walk and not faint."

—Isaiah 40:29~31

The Source of My Strength

The Hiding Place chronicles the life of Corrie ten Boom. Corrie and her family were Dutch believers who hid Jews in their home during the Nazi reign of terror. They were finally arrested and imprisoned for hiding and smuggling Jews to safety. Corrie was the only survivor.

When I consider the condition of the world today—the loss of high moral standards, the increasing instances of violence and drug use, and the basic disregard for human life—I am frightened for us as a nation and am deeply concerned for my children. In a world where rules are scorned and personal rights take precedence over all else, how do I teach my children that some things are worth dying for? Stories like Corrie's help me to keep on keeping on in my own faith walk and to encourage my children in theirs.

Years ago, at the age of twenty-two, a friend encouraged me to enter the Miss America Pageant. I wanted to study professionally in New York City, and the pageant scholarship was substantial enough to make that dream a reality.

But there was a process to it. You had to enter a local pageant first. If you won that, you went on to a state competition. If you won that, you competed in Atlantic City, New Jersey, for the Miss America title. Oh, the effort I put into that endeavor! It took hours, days, months of discipline and perseverance. There were mock interviews, rehearsals, and workouts. There were sessions on walking, wardrobe, cosmetics, and speech. And singing, singing, singing.

Ultimately I won, and I was given many opportunities and blessings as a result of being Miss America. But I did all that for a crown that will perish. How much more should I be willing to do for a crown that is imperishable?

The Bible is filled with stories of men and women who, in the face of impossible circumstances, persevered and were mightily used of God. I want to be the kind of woman God can count on. Yet sometimes I look at my own weaknesses or the circumstances around me and am discouraged. I look at my children and the challenges that could face them and am afraid. But then I lift my eyes to my heavenly Father and am reminded that He is strong.

In *The Hiding Place* Corrie expresses her fear to her father and asks how she can be sure she'll have the courage to walk out her faith if they are caught. Her father says, "Corrie, when we take a train ride, when do you get the ticket to get on the train?" Corrie answered, "When the train is ready to leave." So it is with our God. We need to keep our heart's attitude right, but the ability and strength to persevere come from Him.

Lord, make me a woman of conviction, willing to pay the price and finish the race. When I am weary, remind me that You are the source of my strength.

Perseverance

And we desire that each one of you show the same diligence to the full assurance of hope until the end, that you do not become sluggish, but imitate those who through faith and patience inherit the promises.

HEBREWS 6:11–12

Therefore do not cast away your confidence, which has great reward. For you have need of endurance, so that after you have done the will of God, you may receive the promise.

HEBREWS 10:35–36

In the body of His flesh through death, to present you holy, and blameless, and above reproach in His sight—if indeed you continue in the faith, grounded and steadfast, and are not moved away from the hope of the gospel which you heard, which was preached to every creature under heaven, of which I, Paul, became a minister.

COLOSSIANS 1:22–23

He who overcomes shall be clothed in white garments, and I will not blot out his name from the Book of Life; but I will confess his name before My Father and before His angels.

REVELATION 3:5

As you therefore have received Christ Jesus the Lord, so walk in Him, rooted and built up in Him and established in the faith, as you have been taught, abounding in it with thanksgiving.

COLOSSIANS 2:6–7

Let us hold fast the confession of our hope without wavering, for He who promised is faithful. And let us consider one another in order to stir up love and good works.

HEBREWS 10:23–24

He gives power to the weak,
And to those who have no might
   He increases strength.
Even the youths shall faint and be weary,
And the young men shall utterly fall,
But those who wait on the LORD
Shall renew their strength;
They shall mount up with wings like eagles,

They shall run and not be weary,
They shall walk and not faint.

ISAIAH 40:29–31

For God has not given us a spirit of fear, but of
power and of love and of a sound mind.

2 TIMOTHY 1:7

Be of good courage,
And He shall strengthen your heart,
All you who hope in the LORD.

PSALM 31:24

"So I will strengthen them in the LORD,
And they shall walk up and down in His name,"
Says the LORD.

ZECHARIAH 10:12

Strengthen the weak hands,
And make firm the feeble knees.
Say to those who are fearful-hearted,
"Be strong, do not fear!
Behold, your God will come with vengeance,
With the recompense of God;
He will come and save you."

ISAIAH 35:3–4

In that day the LORD will defend the inhabitants of Jerusalem; the one who is feeble among them in that day shall be like David, and the house of David shall be like God, like the Angel of the LORD before them.

ZECHARIAH 12:8

My Journal Page

Date _____

_____

_____

_____

_____

_____

_____

_____

_____

_____

_____

_____

_____

_____

_____

_____

_____

_____

_____

FINDING HIS WILL

"*For I know the thoughts*

that I think toward you,

says the LORD, *thoughts of peace*

and not of evil, to give you

a future and a hope."

—*Jeremiah 29:11*

Come Out into the Deep

Having our home threatened with foreclosure was a frightening, painful experience. We had built the home ourselves and had intended to live there for many years. We sighed with relief when we had a serious offer from a buyer, and we agreed to a closing date one month before the mortgage holder was to foreclose. Then a new and very real challenge came into focus. We had four children, a dog, a cat, and a goldfish. We had to find someone who would view us as desirable renters. We would have thirty days to pack and move before the closing date. We felt the pressure.

We looked at every house, apartment, and condo in our area. I felt a little like Abraham, packing up my family and belongings without really knowing where we were going. Strangely enough, I felt a real expectancy and anticipation of what God would do. We'd been in limbo for so long, and now, ready or not, the door was closing. I knew that God never closes a door without opening a window.

Within days, a friend who had been renting an old farmhouse near us called to say they were moving out and their home was available. I said yes, sight unseen. We moved into that farmhouse and fell in love with it. Within a couple of months, we were talking about the possibility of buying it, renovating it, and adding on to it as we were able.

But God had other plans. We weren't in that house six months before CBN began to talk to me about moving to Virginia to cohost *The 700 Club*. I really wasn't interested in working full-time. The opportunity to fill in for the full-time cohosts over the last few years had been perfect for me. I was home with my children 95 percent of the time. I was able to be a room mom, go on field trips, bake chocolate-chip cookies—I loved it. Plus, we all loved Milwaukee. We were located between both sets of grandparents and were near extended family. That was important to us. As if all of that wasn't enough, Andy's business was finally taking shape. Surely God wouldn't ask us to walk away from all of that!

As we prayed about it, I uncomfortably remembered telling the Lord when we were first married that we wanted to be risk takers for Him. I began to feel uneasy.

Many years ago I had heard a man teach on the river that flows from beneath the Temple (Ezekiel 47). First God took Ezekiel in up to his ankles, then to his knees, then to his waist, until finally he was out in the deep where he couldn't touch bottom.

That teacher challenged us to advance to a deeper level than where we were. I asked the Lord to take me out to the deep where I would be caught in the current of His purposes and where only He could hold me up. I didn't ask frivolously—I asked with tears flowing and a full sense of my own inadequacy.

In Jeremiah, God promises us a hope and a future, with plans to prosper us. That's just what He promised to Abraham. But there was one condition. Abraham had to do what God wanted him to do. It meant leaving his home and friends and traveling to a new land. It meant walking away from comfort and security. Andy and I began to feel that God was saying, *Come out into the deep!*

In 1993 we left the little farmhouse, our families, and our friends and moved to Virginia. It wasn't easy, but God has been faithful. Change is almost always difficult. Fear of the unknown or an unwillingness to let go of what is secure and controllable can cause us to miss God's plan for our lives. I don't know about you, but I want to be in the center of God's will and caught in the current of His purposes. What level of the river is God calling you into today?

Lord, I am such a creature of habit and comfort. Forgive me when I cling to what is familiar and safe. More than anything, I want to be obedient and available. Give me the courage to come out into the deep where I cannot touch bottom and must trust where You're taking me. When I can't see tomorrow, let me feel Your hand in mine and rest in the knowledge of Your goodness.

In Finding His Will

I will instruct you and teach you in the
   way you should go;
I will guide you with My eye.

PSALM 32:8

Trust in the LORD with all your heart,
And lean not on your own understanding;
In all your ways acknowledge Him,
And He shall direct your paths.

PROVERBS 3:5–6

For I will give you a mouth and wisdom which all
your adversaries will not be able to contradict or
resist.

LUKE 21:15

However, when He, the Spirit of truth, has come,
He will guide you into all truth; for He will not
speak on His own authority, but whatever He hears
He will speak; and He will tell you things to come.

JOHN 16:13

Evil men do not understand justice,
But those who seek the LORD understand all.

PROVERBS 28:5

Turn at my rebuke;
Surely I will pour out my spirit on you;
I will make my words known to you.

PROVERBS 1:23

The entrance of Your words gives light;
It gives understanding to the simple.

PSALM 119:130

Commit your works to the LORD,
And your thoughts will be established.

PROVERBS 16:3

Let us know,
Let us pursue the knowledge of the LORD.
His going forth is established as the morning;
He will come to us like the rain,
Like the latter and former rain to the earth.

HOSEA 6:3

My soul, wait silently for God alone,
For my expectation is from Him.

PSALM 62:5

With Him are wisdom and strength,
He has counsel and understanding.

JOB 12:13

My Journal Page

Date _____

_____

_____

_____

_____

_____

_____

_____

_____

_____

_____

_____

_____

_____

_____

_____

_____

M ATURITY

"My grace is sufficient for you,
for My strength is made perfect
in weakness."

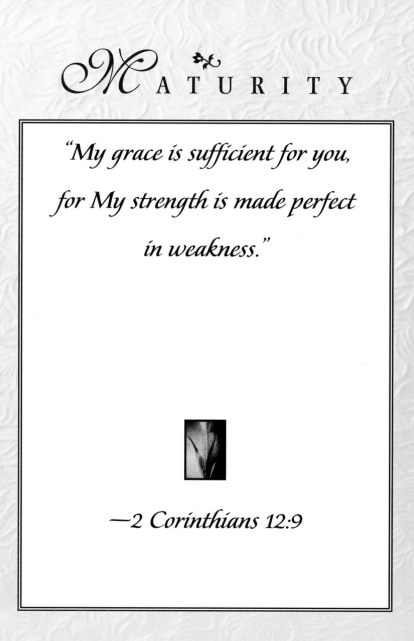

—2 Corinthians 12:9

I Need You

For five years we had the privilege of hosting in our home the most wonderful Bible study group I've ever been a part of.

We started out with about twenty women meeting every Thursday morning. Over the years our numbers grew to well over a hundred, and we finally had to move to a fellowship hall. The women in this group came in all shapes and sizes. There were Protestants, Catholics, charismatics, old and young, black and white, married and single—and all united. We simply hosted the study; Linda Strom taught it.

One Thursday Linda was out of town and had invited Mary Stocking, a local artist and mother of six, to speak. I loved Mary's honesty and humor and sat back knowing I would enjoy her message.

Mary shared how her husband, John, had given her a catamaran for her birthday. Their home is on a large lake, and both Mary and John are active. As they pushed the catamaran into the water, John asked Mary if she wanted him to go out with her. She said no, that she was just fine going out on her own—and off she went. When she was in the middle of the lake, the catamaran capsized and her leg was cut. No matter how hard she tried, Mary could not right that boat. *If I just had someone to help, I could do this,* thought Mary. *If only John were here.* But no one was in sight. She was becoming concerned. *If I hadn't been so proud of my self-sufficiency and so quick to tell John I didn't need him, he'd be out here right now, and I wouldn't be in this situation.*

Then Mary recognized the still, small voice of the Lord: *When you get back to shore, I want you to tell John that you need him.* Mary knew God was speaking to her, not only about her willingness to need John, but also about the importance of verbalizing that so that John knew she needed him.

I was convicted. Andy and I had been married for a number of years and, quite frankly, I prided myself in being pretty self-sufficient. More than that, when there was stress between us, I mentally reveled in the fact that I could handle life on my own if I needed to. I did not want to be vulnerable enough to admit my need.

I want you to tell Andy that you need him. Mary was still speaking, but inside my heart, I heard that directive from the Lord as clearly as if it had been spoken aloud. *No problem. I can do that*, I thought, sure of my own ability again. Do you know that though I tried to tell him every day, it took me *two weeks* to get those words through my lips. Finally, one night in bed, I haltingly explained that there was something I knew the Lord wanted me to tell him and that it was very difficult for me. He listened patiently.

"I, uh, I just wanted you to know that I . . . I need you." There. I'd said it. Andy smiled, squeezed my hand, and said, "That's nice, dear. Thank you." He turned off his reading light and rolled over. I turned off my light, shaking my head and chuckling to myself as I realized what God had always known. Andy didn't need to hear that as much as I needed to acknowledge it.

We need to be *willing* to need each other as husbands, as wives, as families, as friends, and as the body of Christ. When we stand alone we are not stronger, we are diminished. We need one another, even as we need God. My friend and author Sister Francis Clare of Notre Dame puts it this way: "God, help me to be little so You can be big!" Acknowledging our smallness opens the door for God to fill us with His bigness.

Lord, thank You for helping me to see how much I need You. And when I drift back into trying to handle things alone, pull me back to You. Help me to stay little so You can be big.

In Maturity

If any of you lacks wisdom, let him ask of God, who gives to all liberally and without reproach, and it will be given to him.

JAMES 1:5

But grow in the grace and knowledge of our Lord and Savior Jesus Christ. To Him be the glory both now and forever. Amen.

2 PETER 3:18

For though by this time you ought to be teachers, you need someone to teach you again the first principles of the oracles of God; and you have come to need milk and not solid food.

HEBREWS 5:12

Therefore, leaving the discussion of the elementary principles of Christ, let us go on to perfection, not laying again the foundation of repentance from dead works and of faith toward God, of the doctrine of baptisms, of laying on of hands, of resurrection of the dead, and of eternal judgment.

HEBREWS 6:1–2

However, when He, the Spirit of truth, has come, He will guide you into all truth; for He will not speak on His own authority, but whatever He hears He will speak; and He will tell you things to come.

JOHN 16:13

If you seek her as silver,
And search for her as for hidden treasures;
Then you will understand the fear of the LORD,
And find the knowledge of God.
For the LORD gives wisdom;
From His mouth come knowledge
    and understanding;
He stores up sound wisdom for the upright;
He is a shield to those who walk uprightly.

PROVERBS 2:4–7

Now we have received, not the spirit of the world, but the Spirit who is from God, that we might know the things that have been freely given to us by God.

1 CORINTHIANS 2:12

For I will give you a mouth and wisdom which all your adversaries will not be able to contradict or resist.

LUKE 21:15

Being confident of this very thing, that He who has begun a good work in you will complete it until the day of Jesus Christ.

PHILIPPIANS 1:6

Now may the God of peace Himself sanctify you completely; and may your whole spirit, soul, and body be preserved blameless at the coming of our Lord Jesus Christ. He who calls you is faithful, who also will do it.

1 THESSALONIANS 5:23–24

The fear of the LORD is the beginning of wisdom;
A good understanding have all those who do
    His commandments.
His praise endures forever.

PSALM 111:10

I will bring the blind by a way they did not know;
I will lead them in paths they have not known.
I will make darkness light before them,
And crooked places straight.
These things I will do for them,
And not forsake them.

ISAIAH 42:16

With Him are wisdom and strength,
He has counsel and understanding.

JOB 12:13

For if these things are yours and abound, you will
be neither barren nor unfruitful in the knowledge of
our Lord Jesus Christ.

2 PETER 1:8

He shall be like a tree
Planted by the rivers of water,
That brings forth its fruit in its season,
Whose leaf also shall not wither;
And whatever he does shall prosper.

PSALM 1:3

Every branch in Me that does not bear fruit He
takes away; and every branch that bears fruit He
prunes, that it may bear more fruit. . . . I am the
vine, you are the branches. He who abides in Me,
and I in him, bears much fruit; for without Me you
can do nothing.

JOHN 15:2, 5

My Journal Page

Date _____

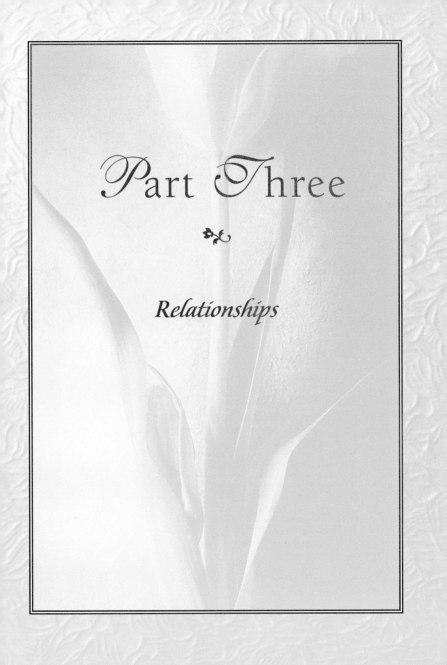

Part Three

❧

Relationships

LONELINESS

"*The* L*ORD* *is my shepherd;*

I shall not want."

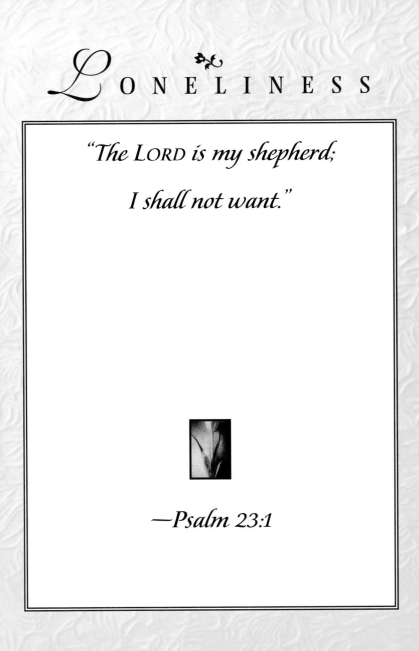

—*Psalm 23:1*

Alone but Not Lonely

One result of being on a daily television program is that people feel that they know you. On *The 700 Club*, where we talk about issues of the heart, I feel that I hardly ever meet a stranger. A feeling of familiarity transcends any awkwardness that might otherwise exist when two strangers meet.

We receive a considerable amount of mail in my office, and much of it is from people whose lives are filled with pain and fear. Many letter writers say, "I've never shared this with anyone before" or "There's no one else I can talk to." The problems differ, but the common thread that runs through them all is loneliness. Men and women in broken marriages, alcoholics, victims of sexual abuse and domestic violence, depressed young people, people with sexual identity problems. People feel trapped and alone.

The Bible is full of people who struggled with loneliness.

Sometimes when we read their stories we feel comfortable with the familiarity of them and don't really consider their extenuating circumstances.

Take Moses for example. We usually think of how God answered the prayers of his mother's heart and how blessed he was to have been plucked out of the Nile by Pharaoh's daughter. But I'm sure he felt the stares and whispers as the only Hebrew in an Egyptian royal household. While he was raised in a privileged environment, his people suffered at the hands of the very man in whose home he lived, at whose table he ate. Talk about an identity crisis!

Moses was a man without a country. When he did move in defense of his people, he wound up killing an Egyptian, being scorned by his people, and fleeing into the desert to escape Pharaoh. Even later in his life, he was still a man called apart for the things of God. He must have been lonely.

Consider Joseph. He was betrayed by his brothers, sold into slavery, and carried off to a foreign country. While there he was unjustly accused, imprisoned, and forgotten. He must have been lonely.

Then there was Esther, a beautiful young Jewish girl. Her parents had died, Mordecai had adopted her, and suddenly she was taken to the palace as part of a harem of women for a very self-centered king. Though she finds favor in his eyes, there is no pledge of fidelity. She must have been lonely.

All of these Bible heroes have their loneliness in common. But they share a more significant trait. They served a God who is great and mighty and who brought them comfort and hope in the midst of their loneliness. What He did for Moses, Joseph, and Esther, He will also do for you.

Father, when I am lonely it is easy to allow depression to get a foothold in my life. Instead of feeling sorry for myself, I choose to lift my voice in praise to You. Fill me with the wonder of who You are and Your great love for me. Forgive me for looking to others for what I can only find in You. You are my all in all.

For Times of Loneliness

I will not leave you orphans; I will come to you.

JOHN 14:18

*F*or I am persuaded that neither death nor life, nor angels nor principalities nor powers, nor things present nor things to come, nor height nor depth, nor any other created thing, shall be able to separate us from the love of God which is in Christ Jesus our Lord.

ROMANS 8:38–39

*C*asting all your care upon Him, for He cares for you.

1 PETER 5:7

*T*he LORD also will be a refuge for the oppressed, A refuge in times of trouble.
And those who know Your name will put their trust in You;
For You, LORD, have not forsaken those who seek You.

PSALM 9:9–10

*L*et your conduct be without covetousness; be content with such things as you have. For He Himself has said, "I will never leave you nor forsake you."

HEBREWS 13:5

*F*ear not, for I am with you;
Be not dismayed, for I am your God.
I will strengthen you,
Yes, I will help you,
I will uphold you with My righteous
    right hand.

ISAIAH 41:10

*W*ho shall separate us from the love of Christ? Shall tribulation, or distress, or persecution, or famine, or nakedness, or peril, or sword? As it is written: "For Your sake we are killed all day long; We are accounted as sheep for the slaughter." Yet in all these things we are more than conquerors through Him who loved us.

ROMANS 8:35–37

*B*e strong and of good courage, do not fear nor be afraid of them; for the LORD your God, He is the

One who goes with you. He will not leave you nor forsake you.

DEUTERONOMY 31:6

"Teaching them to observe all things that I have commanded you; and lo, I am with you always, even to the end of the age." Amen.

MATTHEW 28:20

I will be glad and rejoice in Your mercy,
For You have considered my trouble;
You have known my soul in adversities.

PSALM 31:7

For the people shall dwell in Zion at Jerusalem;
You shall weep no more.
He will be very gracious to you at the sound of
　your cry;
When He hears it, He will answer you.

ISAIAH 30:19

Unto the upright there arises light in the darkness;
He is gracious, and full of compassion,
　and righteous.

PSALM 112:4

$\mathcal{T}$herefore you now have sorrow; but I will see you again and your heart will rejoice, and your joy no one will take from you.

JOHN 16:22

$\mathcal{A}$s a father pities his children,
So the LORD pities those who fear Him.

PSALM 103:13

My Journal Page

Date _____

_____

_____

_____

_____

_____

_____

_____

_____

_____

_____

_____

_____

_____

_____

_____

_____

_____

RELATIONSHIPS

"By this all will know that you are

My disciples, if you have love

for one another."

—John 13:35

Let Love Be Your Greatest Aim

I love weddings. The celebration, the solemnity, the unspoken dream, the gathering of family and friends as two lives come together—each element is an important part of this uniquely special event. While I love seeing all the wonderful, personal touches the bride and groom have chosen to express their love for each other, what I look forward to most is the message the minister or priest shares during the ceremony.

Several years ago, I was asked by some friends in our church to sing at their daughter's wedding. We had moved through the first part of the ceremony and I was settled back in anticipation as our pastor picked up the microphone and turned to the couple. "Patrick and Becky, today I want to talk to you about the importance of keeping courtesy with each other." *Keeping courtesy? How uninspiring.* I wondered where he was going with this. What followed was a message not just for the bride and groom, but for all of us. I've never forgotten it.

The pastor told them to always have each other's best interests at heart. In the first weeks and months of marriage, this comes rather easily. Love causes us to overlook each other's faults, and we are usually attentive to each other's needs. The words *I love you* come easily and often. But in time, we disappoint each other. Resentment and irritation cloud the memory of the special traits that first attracted us.

Most of us know a couple or two who are unpleasant to be around for any length of time because of the way they put each other down. Sometimes one makes a blatant ridiculing comment; sometimes one sneers or delivers an offensive jab. Whether the couple spar with equal ability or one partner sits silently wounded, the relationship is damaged and diminished. Some couples are always civil to each other in public but are rude in private.

This isn't a problem common only to couples. Parents

and children, brothers and sisters, employers and employees—it can happen to any of us if we let it. It can start with teasing meant to be funny—but at someone else's expense. It can be a story of someone else's mistake—without asking ahead of time if we could tell it; or it can be a public reprimand that should have taken place in private.

This is an obedience issue. We have complete freedom to choose how we'll respond to each other. I have the most trouble with this when I'm tired or overwhelmed. Little things irritate me in those moments. Instead of nipping my irritation in the bud, I stew about it. My best friend, Linda Strom, who is in full-time ministry, calls this "stinkin' thinkin'."

Stinkin' thinkin' starts with muttering and, left unrestrained, can build to a self-indulgent crescendo: what I should have said . . . what he should have done . . . how unfair it was . . . how overworked and unappreciated I am . . . if he really cares . . . I had the right-of-way . . . The list is endless.

Stinkin' thinkin' robs our joy and destroys our peace. God has provided a way to avoid it, but we have to *choose* to use it. You'll find it in Philippians 4:8: "Finally, brethren, whatever things are true, whatever things are noble, whatever things are just, whatever things are pure, whatever things are lovely, whatever things are of good report, if there is any virtue and if there is anything praiseworthy—meditate on these things."

Whenever a problem comes up that requires confronting someone, Linda has always said, "Let's let love be our greatest aim," just as Paul exhorts us to "pursue love" (see 1 Corinthians 14:1).

Paul also reminds us of the unique qualities of real love: Love is always patient and kind. It does not demand its own way. It's not irritable or touchy. It does not hold grudges and *hardly notices when others do it wrong.* If you love someone, you're always loyal, you always expect the best of that person, and you always stand your ground in defending that person (see 1 Corinthians 13).

I don't know about you, but I am both convicted and challenged by this description. God says we must do only two things: (1) believe on the name of His Son, Jesus, and (2) love one another.

Lord, help me to reflect Your love in the privacy of my home as well as in the marketplace. When I'm feeling irritable and touchy, remind me of Your forgiving, patient love that You always extend to me. Let Your love flow through me to all You send my way. Teach me to keep courtesy.

In Fellowship

A new commandment I give to you, that you love one another; as I have loved you, that you also love one another. By this all will know that you are My disciples, if you have love for one another.

JOHN 13:34–35

Let the word of Christ dwell in you richly in all wisdom, teaching and admonishing one another in psalms and hymns and spiritual songs, singing with grace in your hearts to the Lord.

COLOSSIANS 3:16

And they continued steadfastly in the apostles' doctrine and fellowship, in the breaking of bread, and in prayers. . . . So continuing daily with one accord in the temple, and breaking bread from house to house, they ate their food with gladness and simplicity of heart, praising God and having favor with all the people. And the Lord added to the church daily those who were being saved.

ACTS 2:42, 46–47

That which we have seen and heard we declare to you, that you also may have fellowship with us; and truly our fellowship is with the Father and with His Son Jesus Christ. . . . But if we walk in the light as He is in the light, we have fellowship with one another, and the blood of Jesus Christ His Son cleanses us from all sin.

1 John 1:3, 7

Then those who feared the Lord spoke to
   one another,
And the Lord listened and heard them;
So a book of remembrance was written before Him
For those who fear the Lord
And who meditate on His name.

Malachi 3:16

That their hearts may be encouraged, being knit together in love, and attaining to all riches of the full assurance of understanding, to the knowledge of the mystery of God, both of the Father and of Christ.

Colossians 2:2

And walk in love, as Christ also has loved us and given Himself for us, an offering and a sacrifice to God for a sweet-smelling aroma.

Ephesians 5:2

We took sweet counsel together,
And walked to the house of God in the throng.

PSALM 55:14

That they all may be one, as You, Father, are in
Me, and I in You; that they also may be one in
Us, that the world may believe that You sent Me.
And the glory which You gave Me I have given
them, that they may be one just as We are one: I
in them, and You in Me; that they may be made
perfect in one, and that the world may know that
You have sent Me, and have loved them as You
have loved Me.

JOHN 17:21–23

As iron sharpens iron,
So a man sharpens the countenance of his friend.

PROVERBS 27:17

God is faithful, by whom you were called into the
fellowship of His Son, Jesus Christ our Lord.

1 CORINTHIANS 1:9

Two are better than one,
Because they have a good reward for their labor.
For if they fall, one will lift up his companion.

But woe to him who is alone when he falls,
For he has no one to help him up.

ECCLESIASTES 4:9–10

*L*et each of us please his neighbor for his good,
leading to edification. . . . May the God of patience
and comfort grant you to be like-minded toward one
another, according to Christ Jesus.

ROMANS 15:2, 5

I have shown you in every way, by laboring like
this, that you must support the weak. And
remember the words of the Lord Jesus, that He said,
"It is more blessed to give than to receive."

ACTS 20:35

My Journal Page

Date _____

_____

_____

_____

_____

_____

_____

_____

_____

_____

_____

_____

_____

_____

_____

_____

_____

_____

_____

 Loving Others

"A new commandment I give to you,

that you love one another;

as I have loved you,

that you also love one another."

—John 13:34

Love Bears All Things

$\mathcal{A}$s a mother I want my children to be gentle and generous of spirit in their evaluation of others. It's easy to be critical of people who are unlovely or annoying; it's inadvertent and spontaneous for us to compare ourselves to people whom we encounter, read about, or even see in the media. This activity leaves us feeling either superior or inferior. How *should* we react to people who are unlovely or annoying to us?

Recently, I took my daughter, Tory, to Atlantic City, New Jersey, for the seventy-fifth anniversary of the Miss America Pageant. A big reunion of former Miss Americas was planned, and forty-four of us were returning. A special book had been commissioned to commemorate the anniversary. Tory went armed with the book and a pen, determined to get every autograph.

As we walked along the boardwalk, I was struck by the incredible dichotomy before us. Flashing lights and glittering displays lit the boardwalk. Pageant attendees were dressed to the nines in tuxedos and dresses that sparkled. In the midst of it all, homeless people curled up alongside the buildings. Beggars, many of them handicapped, were playing harmonicas or holding out hopeful cups.

As I watched my daughter look with admiration and awe at all the "beautiful" people, I prayed, *Lord, help her to see past the trimmings. Teach her to find her identity in You—not in her family or her possessions or her accomplishments. Help us both, as women of God, to see people the way You see them. And, Lord, when we come upon people who've lost track of who they are, help us to slow down and acknowledge them.*

Perhaps the most difficult people to love are those who are rude or unloving to us or to our loved ones. Our gut reaction is to lash back. The Lord has used my children to tame my tongue.

Something happens to me when I get behind the wheel

of my car. My friend Linda laughs and says I'm actually a different person behind the wheel. She's right.

On several occasions (too numerous to mention) when we're en route to some appointment, I've heard one of my children holler from the back of the car, "If that idiot in front of us would step on it, we could all make it through this green light." Ouch! Wonder where he picked that up?!

At moments like those, I realize how closely my children listen to all that I say and watch all that I do. I can read Scripture and lecture consistently to them, but if I'm not living it out, I might as well save my breath.

James 1:22–27 says, "But be doers of the word, and not hearers only, deceiving yourselves. For if anyone is a hearer of the word and not a doer, he is like a man observing his natural face in a mirror; for he observes himself, goes away, and immediately forgets what kind of man he was. But he who looks into the perfect law of liberty and continues in it, and is not a forgetful hearer but a doer of the work, this one will be blessed in what he does. If anyone among you thinks he is religious, and does not bridle his tongue but deceives his own heart, this one's religion is useless. Pure and undefiled religion before God and the Father is this: to visit orphans and widows in their trouble, and to keep oneself unspotted from the world."

It's easy to love the lovely, but speaking gentle words from a kind and forgiving heart when you've been wronged or provoked is a work of the Holy Spirit. It happens when we give up our agenda and grab hold of God's. Jesus said, "A new commandment I give to you, that you love one another; as I have loved you, that you also love one another. By this all will know that you are My disciples, if you have love for one another" (John 13:34–35).

Lord, forgive me for judging others harshly and speaking critically. Help me to remember how much You have forgiven in my own life. I want to reflect You to all I meet, and especially to my children. Use my words to bring wholeness and healing.

In Love of Others

Beloved, if God so loved us, we also ought to love one another. No one has seen God at any time. If we love one another, God abides in us, and His love has been perfected in us.

1 John 4:11–12

Finally, all of you be of one mind, having compassion for one another; love as brothers, be tenderhearted, be courteous; not returning evil for evil or reviling for reviling, but on the contrary blessing, knowing that you were called to this, that you may inherit a blessing.

1 Peter 3:8–9

This is My commandment, that you love one another as I have loved you. Greater love has no one than this, than to lay down one's life for his friends.

John 15:12–13

" And you shall love the Lord your God with all your heart, with all your soul, with all your mind, and with all your strength." This is the first commandment. And the second, like it, is this: "You shall love your neighbor as yourself." There is no other commandment greater than these.

MARK 12:30–31

Though I speak with the tongues of men and of angels, but have not love, I have become sounding brass or a clanging cymbal. And though I have the gift of prophecy, and understand all mysteries and all knowledge, and though I have all faith, so that I could remove mountains, but have not love, I am nothing. And though I bestow all my goods to feed the poor, and though I give my body to be burned, but have not love, it profits me nothing. Love suffers long and is kind; love does not envy; love does not parade itself, is not puffed up; does not behave rudely, does not seek its own, is not provoked, thinks no evil; does not rejoice in iniquity, but rejoices in the truth; bears all things, believes all things, hopes all things, endures all things. Love never fails. But whether there are prophecies, they will fail; whether there are tongues, they will cease; whether there is knowledge, it will vanish away.

1 CORINTHIANS 13:1–8

$\mathcal{B}$y this all will know that you are My disciples, if you have love for one another.

JOHN 13:35

$\mathcal{B}$ut I say to you, love your enemies, bless those who curse you, do good to those who hate you, and pray for those who spitefully use you and persecute you.

MATTHEW 5:44

$\mathcal{A}$nd this commandment we have from Him: that he who loves God must love his brother also.

1 JOHN 4:21

$\mathcal{B}$eloved, do not avenge yourselves, but rather give place to wrath; for it is written, "Vengeance is Mine, I will repay," says the Lord. Therefore
"If your enemy is hungry, feed him;
If he is thirsty, give him a drink;
For in so doing you will heap coals of fire on
    his head."
Do not be overcome by evil, but overcome evil with good.

ROMANS 12:19–21

$\mathcal{S}$ince you have purified your souls in obeying the truth through the Spirit in sincere love of the brethren, love one another fervently with a pure heart.

1 PETER 1:22

Love does no harm to a neighbor; therefore love is the fulfillment of the law.

ROMANS 13:10

Beloved, let us love one another, for love is of God; and everyone who loves is born of God and knows God. He who does not love does not know God, for God is love.

1 JOHN 4:7–8

He who loves his brother abides in the light, and there is no cause for stumbling in him.

1 JOHN 2:10

But do not forget to do good and to share, for with such sacrifices God is well pleased.

HEBREWS 13:16

Behold, how good and how pleasant it is
For brethren to dwell together in unity!
It is like the precious oil upon the head,
Running down on the beard,

The beard of Aaron,
Running down on the edge of his garments.

PSALM 133:1–2

We know that we have passed from death to life, because we love the brethren. He who does not love his brother abides in death. . . . My little children, let us not love in word or in tongue, but in deed and in truth. And by this we know that we are of the truth, and shall assure our hearts before Him.

1 JOHN 3:14, 18–19

For God is not unjust to forget your work and labor of love which you have shown toward His name, in that you have ministered to the saints, and do minister.

HEBREWS 6:10

Finally, brethren, farewell. Become complete. Be of good comfort, be of one mind, live in peace; and the God of love and peace will be with you.

2 CORINTHIANS 13:11

My Journal Page

Date _____

_____

_____

_____

_____

_____

_____

_____

_____

_____

_____

_____

_____

_____

_____

_____

_____

_____

Marriage and Family

"And now abide faith, hope,

love, these three;

but the greatest of these is love."

—1 Corinthians 13:13

Family Matters

The family is the cotter pin of our society. When the family unit is diminished in any way, the repercussions are felt in our whole culture. That's nothing new. Bible stories are filled with the hard-learned lessons that resulted from jealousy, favoritism, disobedience, and manipulations in families. So what do we do? How do we hold on to our families and cling to the principles we know to be true? One thing I am sure of, it doesn't happen just because we have good intentions.

God created us to be relational—first with Him and then with one another. As long as the relationship takes top priority we seem to do well. But eventually, our personal desires and frustrations begin to speak to us more convincingly than the voice of wisdom. Look around you—you'll see it everywhere. Families breaking up because of alchohol, unfaithfulness, pornography. Childeren who've gone into the "far country" of drugs, sex, abortion. I'm talking about Christians—people who love God! How can it be?

I know what I've seen in my own life. I'm going to be as candid as possible with you because I want you to know that the things I am sharing I struggle with myself. When I really look at these situations, the problem is not so much circumstances or other people as it is my own heart attitude. Most sin doesn't come at us with a big red ID tag on it. It sneaks up on us a little at a time, usually when we're offended, wounded, lonely, or afraid. In the Song of Solomon it says it is the "little foxes" that spoil the vineyard. When we give a foot hold to "little foxes," they begin to grow and soon crowd out and consume all the good fruit.

In marriage it is so important to communicate openly and honestly with each other. It's not always easy to do. When I am hurt, frustrated, or irritated, I tend to pull away and get very distant. It is a real challenge for me to lay aside my rights for the sake of the relationship. Yet the Book of

Romans clearly says that to follow Jesus I must die to myself. When I cling to my own rights I become self-seeking and judgmental. Choosing to let go of my irritation and frustration is a real challenge, and it is not without cost.

I worry that we have been selling a cheap gospel lately; not clearly defining the cost of being commited to Chirst. Galatians 2:20 says, "I have been crucified with Christ; it is no longer I who live, but Christ lives in me; and the life which I now live in the flesh I live by faith in the Son of God, who loved me and gave Himself for me." In other words, my agenda and my rights were nailed to the cross with Christ when I committed my life to Him. Dying to self is a daily choice that is never more challenged than in my relationships with others.

When the enemy can't find a way to attack me personally, you can bet the next place he'll try is my relationships with others. By staying in God's Word, praying, and routing out those "little foxes" whenever they appear, we build a wall of protection around our hearts and our loved ones. It's not something we do once and are done with. It requires vigilance!

Sometimes, even when I'm in the word and praying, I need to ask the Lord to give me the strength and the willingness to let go of my way and grab hold of His. If I wait too long in giving up control I begin to rationalize truth and make excuses for my behavior and eventually I no longer hear God speaking. Sadly enough, all around me today, I know of relationships so damaged and unattended to that the people involved no longer *want* God to restore them.

Jesus said we are the salt of the earth and the light of the world. We are to season the world with the flavor of our faith and pierce the darkness of sin with the light of truth in our hearts. When we allow discord and division in our marriages or families we are building our house on sand. When the rains descend, and the floods come, and the winds blow, it will fall. But the house that is built on the rock will remain standing.

🌿

Lord, help me to love my husband and my children unconditionally like You love me. It's so easy for me to say that and so hard for me to do it. I willingly lay down my "rights" to You. Have Your way in me, O God. Make me a "light bearer" in my household. Help me to reflect You to my family.

Family

So they said, "Believe on the Lord Jesus Christ, and you will be saved, you and your household."

ACTS 16:31

And if it seems evil to you to serve the LORD, choose for yourselves this day whom you will serve, whether the gods which your fathers served that were on the other side of the River, or the gods of the Amorites, in whose land you dwell. But as for me and my house, we will serve the LORD.

JOSHUA 24:15

Train up a child in the way he should go, And when he is old he will not depart from it.

PROVERBS 22:6

Honor your father and your mother, that your days may be long upon the land which the LORD your God is giving you.

EXODUS 20:12

Wives, submit to your own husbands, as to the Lord. For the husband is head of the wife, as also

Christ is head of the church; and He is the Savior of the body. Therefore, just as the church is subject to Christ, so let the wives be to their own husbands in everything. Husbands, love your wives, just as Christ also loved the church and gave Himself for her, that He might sanctify and cleanse her with the washing of water by the word, that He might present her to Himself a glorious church, not having spot or wrinkle or any such thing, but that she should be holy and without blemish. So husbands ought to love their own wives as their own bodies; he who loves his wife loves himself. For no one ever hated his own flesh, but nourishes and cherishes it, just as the Lord does the church. For we are members of His body, of His flesh and of His bones. "For this reason a man shall leave his father and mother and be joined to his wife, and the two shall become one flesh." This is a great mystery, but I speak concerning Christ and the church. Nevertheless let each one of you in particular so love his own wife as himself, and let the wife see that she respects her husband.

Children, obey your parents in the Lord, for this is right. "Honor your father and mother," which is the first commandment with promise: "that it may be well with you and you may live long on the earth." And you, fathers, do not provoke your children to wrath, but bring them up in the training and admonition of the Lord.

EPHESIANS 5:22–6:4

One who rules his own house well, having his children in submission with all reverence (for if a man does not know how to rule his own house, how will he take care of the church of God?).

1 TIMOTHY 3:4–5

Behold, children are a heritage from the LORD,
The fruit of the womb is a reward.
Like arrows in the hand of a warrior,
So are the children of one's youth.
Happy is the man who has his quiver full of them;
They shall not be ashamed,
But shall speak with their enemies in the gate.

PSALM 127:3–5

And he will turn
The hearts of the fathers to the children,
And the hearts of the children to their fathers,
Lest I come and strike the earth with a curse.

MALACHI 4:6

Children's children are the crown of old men,
And the glory of children is their father.

And these words which I command you today
shall be in your heart. You shall teach them
diligently to your children, and shall talk of them
when you sit in your house, when you walk by the
way, when you lie down, and when you rise up. You
shall bind them as a sign on your hand, and they
shall be as frontlets between your eyes. You shall
write them on the doorposts of your house and on
your gates.

DEUTERONOMY 6:6–9

Correct your son, and he will give you rest;
Yes, he will give delight to your soul.

PROVERBS 29:17

And you, fathers, do not provoke your children to
wrath, but bring them up in the training and
admonition of the Lord.

EPHESIANS 6:4

A good man leaves an inheritance to his
children's children,

But the wealth of the sinner is stored up for
  the righteous.

PROVERBS 13:22

Blessed is every one who fears the LORD,
Who walks in His ways.
When you eat the labor of your hands,
You shall be happy, and it shall be well with you.
Your wife shall be like a fruitful vine
In the very heart of your house,
Your children like olive plants
All around your table.
Behold, thus shall the man be blessed
Who fears the LORD.

PSALM 128:1–4

The father of the righteous will greatly rejoice,
And he who begets a wise child will delight in him.

PROVERBS 23:24

All your children shall be taught by the LORD,
And great shall be the peace of your children.

ISAIAH 54:13

My Journal Page

Date _____

_____

_____

_____

_____

_____

_____

_____

_____

_____

_____

_____

_____

_____

_____

_____

_____

WITNESSING

"Freely you have received,

freely give."

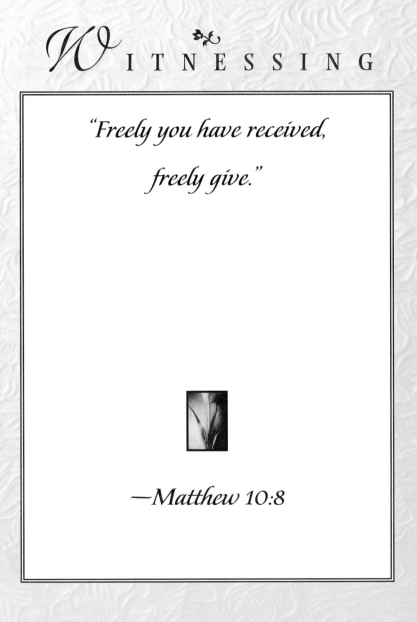

—Matthew 10:8

Sharing Our Faith

As much as I enjoy Linda Strom's teaching, I love her gift for evangelism even more. For Linda, sharing Jesus is as natural as breathing. She never forgets, she never gets sidetracked, she never gets tired of sharing the love of God.

That's the way I want to be, but often busyness, weariness, or fear of rejection gets in the way. About a year ago, a friend was experiencing some difficulties in her marriage. I commiserated with her, offered sympathetic advice, and walked away. I felt her frustration and hopelessness. Later that day I began to pray for her when the Lord gently chided me. *Why didn't you tell her about Me?*

We often listen to people's pain, frustration, and anger, yet we never give them an understanding of who God is and what He wants to do in our lives. As I reflected on my conversation with my friend, I realized that I had not shared anything with her that would meet her need. I knew the

One who was the answer to her problem and had failed to share Him.

As cohost of *The 700 Club*, I have the incredible privilege of sharing the love of God and His plan for our salvation with millions of people every single day. That privilege is awesome, and I do not take it for granted. But I lost the burden and urgency for the souls of people around me—the burden that kept me praying and waiting for God to open an opportunity. I've asked the Lord to rekindle that burden in me for my neighbors, my children's friends, and the clerks, service people, and others God brings my way.

The hardest situation we encounter in sharing our faith occurs when we desperately want to see someone in our family come to a saving knowledge of Jesus. It requires wisdom and perseverance.

I've learned from experience that people are more often won by the consistency of our lifestyles than by our theological expounding. Sometimes God opens opportunities immediately. Usually, however, we earn the right to speak candidly only after investing ourselves in relationships with genuine caring and sincere interest.

If you've been sharing and getting nowhere, be still—pray! The Bible says the Spirit of God woos the heart, preparing it to hear and receive the great good news. Therefore, pray without ceasing and beseech the Holy Spirit to touch the hearts of your family, your neighbors, your friends. "Now may the God of peace who brought up our Lord Jesus from the dead, that great Shepherd of the sheep, through the blood of the everlasting covenant, make you complete in every good work to do His will, working in you what is well pleasing in His sight, through Jesus Christ, to whom be glory forever and ever. Amen" (Hebrews 13:20–21).

Lord my heart is burdened for my family and friends. I pray that my life will reflect Your goodness and love. And when I am able to speak of You, let my voice be gentle and my attitude winsome. Give me Your heart for the lost.

In Witness

And Jesus came and spoke to them, saying, "All authority has been given to Me in heaven and on earth. Go therefore and make disciples of all the nations, baptizing them in the name of the Father and of the Son and of the Holy Spirit, teaching them to observe all things that I have commanded you; and lo, I am with you always, even to the end of the age." Amen.

MATTHEW 28:18–20

And He said to them, "Go into all the world and preach the gospel to every creature."

MARK 16:15

You therefore, my son, be strong in the grace that is in Christ Jesus. And the things that you have heard from me among many witnesses, commit these to faithful men who will be able to teach others also.

2 TIMOTHY 2:1–2

Then He said to them, "Thus it is written, and thus it was necessary for the Christ to suffer and to rise from the dead the third day, and that repentance and remission of sins should be preached in His name to all nations, beginning at Jerusalem. And you are witnesses of these things."

LUKE 24:46–48

And He said to them, "It is not for you to know times or seasons which the Father has put in His own authority. But you shall receive power when the Holy Spirit has come upon you; and you shall be witnesses to Me in Jerusalem, and in all Judea and Samaria, and to the end of the earth."

ACTS 1:7–8

Those who are wise shall shine
Like the brightness of the firmament,
And those who turn many to righteousness
Like the stars forever and ever.

DANIEL 12:3

But sanctify the Lord God in your hearts, and always be ready to give a defense to everyone who asks you a reason for the hope that is in you, with meekness and fear; having a good conscience, that when they defame you as evildoers, those who revile your good conduct in Christ may be ashamed.

1 PETER 3:15–16

And you became followers of us and of the Lord, having received the word in much affliction, with joy of the Holy Spirit, so that you became examples to all in Macedonia and Achaia who believe. For from you the word of the Lord has sounded forth, not only in Macedonia and Achaia, but also in every place. Your faith toward God has gone out, so that we do not need to say anything.

1 THESSALONIANS 1:6–8

Ask of Me, and I will give You
The nations for Your inheritance,
And the ends of the earth for Your possession.

PSALM 2:8

And I, if I am lifted up from the earth, will draw all peoples to Myself.

JOHN 12:32

And since we have the same spirit of faith, according to what is written, "I believed and therefore I spoke," we also believe and therefore speak.

2 CORINTHIANS 4:13

Restore to me the joy of Your salvation,
And uphold me by Your generous Spirit.

Then I will teach transgressors Your ways,
And sinners shall be converted to You.

PSALM 51:12–13

Indeed I have given him as a witness to the people,
A leader and commander for the people.
Surely you shall call a nation you do not know,
And nations who do not know you shall run to you,
Because of the LORD your God,
And the Holy One of Israel;
For He has glorified you.

ISAIAH 55:4–5

Now we exhort you, brethren, warn those who are
unruly, comfort the fainthearted, uphold the weak,
be patient with all.

1 THESSALONIANS 5:14

Now it shall come to pass in the latter days
That the mountain of the LORD's house
Shall be established on the top of the mountains,
And shall be exalted above the hills;
And all nations shall flow to it.
Many people shall come and say,
"Come, and let us go up to the mountain
    of the LORD,

To the house of the God of Jacob;
He will teach us His ways,
And we shall walk in His paths."
For out of Zion shall go forth the law,
And the word of the LORD from Jerusalem.

ISAIAH 2:2–3

And this gospel of the kingdom will be preached in all the world as a witness to all the nations, and then the end will come.

MATTHEW 24:14

My Journal Page

Date _____

_____

_____

_____

_____

_____

_____

_____

_____

_____

_____

_____

_____

_____

_____

_____

_____

_____

Part Four

In Difficult Times

DISCOURAGEMENT AND DEPRESSION

"I waited patiently for the LORD;
And He inclined to me,
And heard my cry.
He also brought me up out of a horrible pit,
Out of the miry clay,
And set my feet upon a rock,
And established my steps.
He has put a new song in my mouth—
Praise to our God;
Many will see it and fear,
And will trust in the LORD."

Psalm 40:1–3

The God of a Second Chance

❦

I began working in television in Milwaukee in 1978. While I'd never set out to do talk TV, I felt at home from the beginning, and being in the public eye gave me many opportunities to share my faith. Because it was fairly common knowledge in the community that I was a Christian, the publicity of going through a divorce was difficult. I felt as if I were sitting naked on top of a flagpole in downtown Milwaukee. That winter, I went home at the end of each day to a cold, silent house. Emotionally depressed and grieved, I would then climb into bed with my hat, coat, and boots still on and sleep till morning.

I'm not sure when that heavy veil of grief and emptiness began to lift. But sometime that spring, I became aware of the sweet smell of the wet earth beginning to thaw, the songs of promise that were being sung with such abandon from every nest and perch. I began to move on. I had no intention of dating and no interest in pursuing a new relationship. Though I loved children, I had accepted that there would be none in my first marriage. I was in my thirties, and the prospect of marriage and a family seemed remote and unlikely. Yet God had other plans.

I met Andy Friedrich at a retirement celebration for a coworker. He had gone through a divorce a number of years before that, and after much floundering and searching, a friend had led him to Christ. But no one had discipled him, so he had little knowledge of the Scriptures and wasn't in a church or study group of any kind. Initially we met to talk about the Lord. In time, I grudgingly conceded to a date, but not without apprehension.

Even though Andy was ready for a relationship, I was still gun-shy—so he simply waited. With tenderness and kindness and an incredible amount of patience, he broke down any barriers I'd put up. He was faithful, trustworthy, and committed to the Lord and to me. We were married a little more than a year after we'd begun dating.

The Lord has used Andy in many ways to help heal old wounds in me. He offered both of us a new beginning, a clean slate, a hope, and a future. And I'm now a mom—not once, not twice, but four times over, three sons and a daughter, each a precious, unique gift from the Lord. God has surely given me more than I could hope for or ask.

The story of Joseph in the book of Genesis is one of my favorites. Sold by his brothers into slavery, taken to a foreign land, unfairly accused and imprisoned, and with little hope or expectation of ever seeing his family again, Joseph was in what seemed an impossible situation. Despite all that, the Bible says, "the Lord was with him."

God allowed the testing to build character in Joseph. Joseph went through years of waiting and suffering before he saw God's plan in it all. God used Joseph to save Egypt, the surrounding nations, and Joseph's own family. God's plans and purposes are so much bigger and greater than our own.

At the end of his story, Joseph says, "You meant evil against me; but God meant it for good, in order to bring it about as it is this day" (Genesis 50:20). That same truth is reconfirmed in the book of Romans in the New Testament. "All things work together for good to those who love God" (8:28). God is, indeed, the God of second chances.

❧

Thank You, Lord for the constant message of restoration that runs throughout Your Word. Thank You for the glimpse of Your handiwork that is so much bigger and more beautiful than I could have imagined. Help me to be faithful in times of testing. Align my life with Your will. Spirit of the living God, fall fresh on me.

For Times of Discouragement

Therefore do not cast away your confidence, which has great reward. For you have need of endurance, so that after you have done the will of God, you may receive the promise.

HEBREWS 10:35–36

Being confident of this very thing, that He who has begun a good work in you will complete it until the day of Jesus Christ.

PHILIPPIANS 1:6

And let us not grow weary while doing good, for in due season we shall reap if we do not lose heart.

GALATIANS 6:9

I would have lost heart, unless I had believed
That I would see the goodness of the LORD
In the land of the living.
Wait on the LORD;
Be of good courage,
And He shall strengthen your heart;
Wait, I say, on the LORD!

PSALM 27:13–14

So the ransomed of the LORD shall return,
And come to Zion with singing,
With everlasting joy on their heads.
They shall obtain joy and gladness;
Sorrow and sighing shall flee away.

ISAIAH 51:11

Be anxious for nothing, but in everything by
prayer and supplication, with thanksgiving, let your
requests be made known to God; and the peace of
God, which surpasses all understanding, will guard
your hearts and minds through Christ Jesus.

PHILIPPIANS 4:6–7

In this you greatly rejoice, though now for a
little while, if need be, you have been grieved
by various trials, that the genuineness of your
faith, being much more precious than gold that
perishes, though it is tested by fire, may be found
to praise, honor, and glory at the revelation of
Jesus Christ, whom having not seen you love.
Though now you do not see Him, yet believing,
you rejoice with joy inexpressible and full of glory,
receiving the end of your faith—the salvation of
your souls.

1 PETER 1:6–9

We are hard-pressed on every side, yet not crushed; we are perplexed, but not in despair; persecuted, but not forsaken; struck down, but not destroyed.

2 CORINTHIANS 4:8–9

Though I walk in the midst of trouble, You will
    revive me;
You will stretch out Your hand
Against the wrath of my enemies,
And Your right hand will save me.

PSALM 138:7

Let not your heart be troubled; you believe in God, believe also in Me. . . . Peace I leave with you, My peace I give to you; not as the world gives do I give to you. Let not your heart be troubled, neither let it be afraid.

JOHN 14:1, 27

Be of good courage,
And He shall strengthen your heart,
All you who hope in the LORD.

PSALM 31:24

As a father pities his children,
So the LORD pities those who fear Him.

For He knows our frame;
He remembers that we are dust.

PSALM 103:13–14

The eternal God is your refuge,
And underneath are the everlasting arms;
He will thrust out the enemy from before you,
And will say, "Destroy!"

DEUTERONOMY 33:27

Behold, God will not cast away the blameless,
Nor will He uphold the evildoers.

JOB 8:20

But know that the LORD has set apart for Himself
    him who is godly;
The LORD will hear when I call to Him.

PSALM 4:3

For You, O LORD, will bless the righteous;
With favor You will surround him as with a shield.

PSALM 5:12

But now, thus says the LORD, who created you,
    O Jacob,
And He who formed you, O Israel:

"Fear not, for I have redeemed you;
I have called you by your name;
You are Mine."

ISAIAH 43:1

So he answered, "Do not fear, for those who are
with us are more than those who are with them."

2 KINGS 6:16

For the LORD loves justice,
And does not forsake His saints;
They are preserved forever,
But the descendants of the wicked shall be
    cut off. . . .
Wait on the LORD,
And keep His way,
And He shall exalt you to inherit the land;
When the wicked are cut off, you shall see it.

PSALM 37:28, 34

Let us know,
Let us pursue the knowledge of the LORD.
His going forth is established as the morning;
He will come to us like the rain,
Like the latter and former rain to the earth.

HOSEA 6:3

So Jesus answered and said, "Assuredly, I say to you, there is no one who has left house or brothers or sisters or father or mother or wife or children or lands, for My sake and the gospel's, who shall not receive a hundredfold now in this time—houses and brothers and sisters and mothers and children and lands, with persecutions—and in the age to come, eternal life.

MARK 10:29–30

For Times of Depression

Likewise the Spirit also helps in our weaknesses. For we do not know what we should pray for as we ought, but the Spirit Himself makes intercession for us with groanings which cannot be uttered. Now He who searches the hearts knows what the mind of the Spirit is, because He makes intercession for the saints according to the will of God.

ROMANS 8:26–27

To console those who mourn in Zion,
To give them beauty for ashes,
The oil of joy for mourning,

The garment of praise for the spirit of heaviness;
That they may be called trees of righteousness,
The planting of the LORD, that He may be glorified.

ISAIAH 61:3

Finally, brethren, whatever things are true, whatever things are noble, whatever things are just, whatever things are pure, whatever things are lovely, whatever things are of good report, if there is any virtue and if there is anything praiseworthy—meditate on these things.

PHILIPPIANS 4:8

Therefore humble yourselves under the mighty hand of God, that He may exalt you in due time, casting all your care upon Him, for He cares for you.

1 PETER 5:6–7

Then He spoke a parable to them, that men always ought to pray and not lose heart.

LUKE 18:1

Beloved, do not think it strange concerning the fiery trial which is to try you, as though some strange thing happened to you; but rejoice to the extent that you partake of Christ's sufferings, that

when His glory is revealed, you may also be glad
with exceeding joy.

1 PETER 4:12–13

For His anger is but for a moment,
His favor is for life;
Weeping may endure for a night,
But joy comes in the morning.

PSALM 30:5

Fear not, for I am with you;
Be not dismayed, for I am your God.
I will strengthen you,
Yes, I will help you,
I will uphold you with My righteous right hand.

ISAIAH 41:10

So the ransomed of the LORD shall return,
And come to Zion with singing,
With everlasting joy on their heads.
They shall obtain joy and gladness;
Sorrow and sighing shall flee away.

ISAIAH 51:11

I will not leave you orphans; I will come to you.

JOHN 14:18

When you pass through the waters, I will be
   with you;
And through the rivers, they shall not overflow you.
When you walk through the fire, you shall not
   be burned,
Nor shall the flame scorch you.

ISAIAH 43:2

He heals the brokenhearted
And binds up their wounds.

PSALM 147:3

But I fear, lest somehow, as the serpent deceived
Eve by his craftiness, so your minds may be
corrupted from the simplicity that is in Christ. For if
he who comes preaches another Jesus whom we
have not preached, or if you receive a different spirit
which you have not received, or a different gospel
which you have not accepted—you may well put up
with it!

2 CORINTHIANS 11:3–4

For I am persuaded that neither death nor life,
nor angels nor principalities nor powers, nor things
present nor things to come, nor height nor depth,

nor any other created thing, shall be able to
separate us from the love of God which is in Christ
Jesus our Lord.

ROMANS 8:38–39

The eyes of the LORD are on the righteous,
And His ears are open to their cry. . . .
The righteous cry out, and the LORD hears,
And delivers them out of all their troubles.

PSALM 34:15, 17

Can a woman forget her nursing child,
And not have compassion on the son of her womb?
Surely they may forget,
Yet I will not forget you.
See, I have inscribed you on the palms of My hands;
Your walls are continually before Me.

ISAIAH 49:15–16

Blessed is the man who trusts in the LORD,
And whose hope is the LORD.
For he shall be like a tree planted by the waters,
Which spreads out its roots by the river,
And will not fear when heat comes;
But its leaf will be green,

And will not be anxious in the year of drought,
Nor will cease from yielding fruit.

JEREMIAH 17:7–8

And God will wipe away every tear from their eyes; there shall be no more death, nor sorrow, nor crying. There shall be no more pain, for the former things have passed away.

REVELATION 21:4

My Journal Page

Date _____

TROUBLE AND SUFFERING

"Therefore do not worry, saying,
'What shall we eat?' or
'What shall we drink?' or
'What shall we wear?'...
But seek first the kingdom of God
and His righteousness, and all
these things shall be added to you."

—Matthew 6:31, 33

For Everything There Is a Season

*W*inter in Wisconsin is not for the fainthearted. Yet despite below-zero temperatures, wind, and snow, I love the stark beauty of the season. There's nothing quite like a quiet winter evening—the sound of logs crackling in the fireplace, a soothing cup of Christmas tea, and huge, lacy snowflakes silently blanketing the earth. Moments like these give me a sense of well-being and peace. But one particular January, I was feeling anything but peaceful.

A series of unexpected financial setbacks a couple of years earlier had devoured all of our savings and pushed us deeply into debt. The stress was constant. We were behind in paying many of our bills. An honest mistake in our tax estimate had created thousands of dollars in fines and interest. Our situation only seemed to get worse.

The winter seemed as gray and bleak as our financial

picture. As frustrating as it was to be so in debt, and as tiring as it was to have to watch every penny, the most difficult thing for me as a mother was not being able to give my children simple things.

My oldest son, Drew, was eight years old and (to our chagrin) a big fan of WWF wrestling. He had asked me to buy some ice cream bars shaped like wrestling figures. After each grocery trip, I would honestly report that I could not find them. But even if I had found them, we couldn't afford to buy them. As it was, the pantry was almost bare.

I was folding laundry when the doorbell rang. Karen, a friend from our Thursday morning Bible study, was standing there with a mischievous grin on her face. "We have a surprise for you. Patsy and I were at the Food Pantry picking up food for needy families and we said, 'Why not Terry and Andy?' Please accept this as from the Lord." At that, they began hauling in boxes of food. I was speechless as I realized they had no idea how empty my pantry was.

Just before leaving, Karen pointed to a large box on the

floor. "You'll want to unpack this one first. It's full of frozen things." With that, they were gone as quickly as they'd come. I opened the box of frozen food and what do you think I found? *Boxes* of wrestling-figure ice cream bars! I was astonished! "Lord, how could they know? What would make them choose those specific bars for me?" In the quiet of my heart, I felt the Lord say, *Now, I'm going to show you what it's like when I provide for you.* And He did—week after week, month after month, for several years. In the most unexpected and generous ways, family and friends sustained us with food, clothing, money, and prayers. We were deeply grateful, but it was humbling. "Lord, we've tithed faithfully over and above what You've asked. We've always loved giving. Why have You taken away this blessing?" Lovingly but firmly, the Lord spoke. *You have given faithfully and know the blessing therein. Now, I am blessing others as they give to you, and I want you to learn to receive graciously and humbly. For everything there is a season.*

As difficult as that season was for us, we learned some

valuable lessons. Being willing to receive was as important as being willing to give. Finding our security in Christ rather than in our own ability was painful and humbling.

We began to learn the fine art of contentment. In our kitchen we now have a cherished plaque that reads, CONTENTMENT IS NOT THE FULFILLMENT OF WHAT YOU WANT, BUT THE REALIZATION OF HOW MUCH YOU ALREADY HAVE. The apostle Paul puts it this way, "I have learned in whatever state I am, to be content. . . . I can do all things through Christ who strengthens me" (Philippians 4:11, 13).

Lord, when I'm in a difficult season that I can't control, I see how much I rely on myself. Teach me how to rest in You in the midst of difficulty and change. Jesus, fashion in me the kind of servant's heart that is as able to receive as it is to give. Thank You for Your faithfulness to supply all my needs.

For Times of Trouble

Let not your heart be troubled; you believe in God, believe also in Me. . . . Peace I leave with you, My peace I give to you; not as the world gives do I give to you. Let not your heart be troubled, neither let it be afraid.

John 14:1, 27

For this cause everyone who is godly shall pray
   to You
In a time when You may be found;
Surely in a flood of great waters
They shall not come near him.
You are my hiding place;
You shall preserve me from trouble;
You shall surround me with songs of deliverance.
Selah

Psalm 32:6–7

God is our refuge and strength,
A very present help in trouble.
Therefore we will not fear,
Even though the earth be removed,

And though the mountains be carried into the
  midst of the sea;
Though its waters roar and be troubled,
Though the mountains shake with its swelling.
Selah

PSALM 46:1–3

We are hard-pressed on every side, yet not
crushed; we are perplexed, but not in despair;
persecuted, but not forsaken; struck down, but not
destroyed.

2 CORINTHIANS 4:8–9

Blessed be the God and Father of our Lord Jesus
Christ, the Father of mercies and God of all comfort,
who comforts us in all our tribulation, that we may
be able to comfort those who are in any trouble,
with the comfort with which we ourselves are
comforted by God.

2 CORINTHIANS 1:3–4

Though he fall, he shall not be utterly cast down;
For the LORD upholds him with His hand. . . .
But the salvation of the righteous is from the LORD;
He is their strength in the time of trouble.

PSALM 37:24, 39

The wicked is ensnared by the transgression of
    his lips,
But the righteous will come through trouble. . . .
No grave trouble will overtake the righteous,
But the wicked shall be filled with evil.

Proverbs 12:13, 21

Blessed is he who considers the poor;
The Lord will deliver him in time of trouble.

Psalm 41:1

Though I walk in the midst of trouble, You
    will revive me;
You will stretch out Your hand
Against the wrath of my enemies,
And Your right hand will save me.

Psalm 138:7

He shall deliver you in six troubles,
Yes, in seven no evil shall touch you.

Job 5:19

Then they cried out to the Lord in their trouble,
And He saved them out of their distresses.

Psalm 107:19

The LORD is good,
A stronghold in the day of trouble;
And He knows those who trust in Him.

NAHUM 1:7

And we know that all things work together for
good to those who love God, to those who are the
called according to His purpose.

ROMANS 8:28

Therefore I say to you, do not worry about your
life, what you will eat or what you will drink; nor
about your body, what you will put on. Is not life
more than food and the body more than clothing?
Look at the birds of the air, for they neither sow nor
reap nor gather into barns; yet your heavenly Father
feeds them. Are you not of more value than they?
Which of you by worrying can add one cubit to his
stature? So why do you worry about clothing?
Consider the lilies of the field, how they grow: they
neither toil nor spin; and yet I say to you that even
Solomon in all his glory was not arrayed like one of
these. Now if God so clothes the grass of the field,
which today is, and tomorrow is thrown into the
oven, will He not much more clothe you, O you of
little faith? Therefore do not worry, saying, "What

shall we eat?" or "What shall we drink?" or "What shall we wear?" For after all these things the Gentiles seek. For your heavenly Father knows that you need all these things. But seek first the kingdom of God and His righteousness, and all these things shall be added to you. Therefore do not worry about tomorrow, for tomorrow will worry about its own things. Sufficient for the day is its own trouble.

MATTHEW 6:25–34

For Times of Suffering

For as the sufferings of Christ abound in us, so our consolation also abounds through Christ. . . . And our hope for you is steadfast, because we know that as you are partakers of the sufferings, so also you will partake of the consolation.

2 CORINTHIANS 1:5, 7

These things I have spoken to you, that in Me you may have peace. In the world you will have tribulation; but be of good cheer, I have overcome the world.

JOHN 16:33

Beloved, do not think it strange concerning the fiery trial which is to try you, as though some strange thing happened to you; but rejoice to the extent that you partake of Christ's sufferings, that when His glory is revealed, you may also be glad with exceeding joy. If you are reproached for the name of Christ, blessed are you, for the Spirit of glory and of God rests upon you. On their part He is blasphemed, but on your part He is glorified.

1 PETER 4:12–14

For this is commendable, if because of conscience toward God one endures grief, suffering wrongfully. For what credit is it if, when you are beaten for your faults, you take it patiently? But when you do good and suffer, if you take it patiently, this is commendable before God. For to this you were called, because Christ also suffered for us, leaving us an example, that you should follow His steps.

1 PETER 2:19–21

We are confident, yes, well pleased rather to be absent from the body and to be present with the Lord. Therefore we make it our aim, whether present or absent, to be well pleasing to Him. For we must all appear before the judgment seat of Christ, that each one may receive the things done in the body, according to what he has done, whether good or bad.

2 CORINTHIANS 5:8–10

Is anyone among you suffering? Let him pray. Is anyone cheerful? Let him sing psalms.

JAMES 5:13

The Spirit Himself bears witness with our spirit that we are children of God, and if children, then heirs—heirs of God and joint heirs with Christ, if indeed we suffer with Him, that we may also be glorified together. For I consider that the sufferings of this present time are not worthy to be compared with the glory which shall be revealed in us.

ROMANS 8:16–18

For He has not despised nor abhorred the
    affliction of the afflicted;
Nor has He hidden His face from Him;
But when He cried to Him, He heard.

PSALM 22:24

Wait on the LORD;
Be of good courage,
And He shall strengthen your heart;
Wait, I say, on the LORD!

PSALM 27:14

Cast your burden on the LORD,
And He shall sustain you;
He shall never permit the righteous to be moved.

PSALM 55:22

For a righteous man may fall seven times
And rise again,
But the wicked shall fall by calamity.

PROVERBS 24:16

And the LORD said: "I have surely seen the
oppression of My people who are in Egypt, and have
heard their cry because of their taskmasters, for I
know their sorrows."

EXODUS 3:7

My flesh and my heart fail;
But God is the strength of my heart and my
    portion forever.

PSALM 73:26

The LORD upholds all who fall,
And raises up all who are bowed down.

PSALM 145:14

For the Lord will not cast off forever.
Though He causes grief,
Yet He will show compassion
According to the multitude of His mercies.
For He does not afflict willingly,
Nor grieve the children of men.

LAMENTATIONS 3:31–33

O LORD, my strength and my fortress,
My refuge in the day of affliction,
The Gentiles shall come to You
From the ends of the earth and say,
"Surely our fathers have inherited lies,
Worthlessness and unprofitable things."

JEREMIAH 16:19

No grave trouble will overtake the righteous,
But the wicked shall be filled with evil.

PROVERBS 12:21

For His anger is but for a moment,
His favor is for life;

Weeping may endure for a night,
But joy comes in the morning.

PSALM 30:5

Many are the afflictions of the righteous,
But the LORD delivers him out of them all.

PSALM 34:19

Why are you cast down, O my soul?
And why are you disquieted within me?
Hope in God;
For I shall yet praise Him,
The help of my countenance and my God.

PSALM 42:11

You, who have shown me great and
   severe troubles,
Shall revive me again,
And bring me up again from the depths of the earth.

PSALM 71:20

For You will save the humble people,
But will bring down haughty looks.
For You will light my lamp;
The LORD my God will enlighten my darkness.

PSALM 18:27–28

Those who sow in tears
Shall reap in joy.
He who continually goes forth weeping,
Bearing seed for sowing,
Shall doubtless come again with rejoicing,
Bringing his sheaves with him.

PSALM 126:5–6

For Times of Bereavement

But I do not want you to be ignorant, brethren, concerning those who have fallen asleep, lest you sorrow as others who have no hope. For if we believe that Jesus died and rose again, even so God will bring with Him those who sleep in Jesus.

1 THESSALONIANS 4:13–14

And God will wipe away every tear from their eyes; there shall be no more death, nor sorrow, nor crying. There shall be no more pain, for the former things have passed away.

REVELATION 21:4

Now He who has prepared us for this very thing is God, who also has given us the Spirit as a guarantee. So we are always confident, knowing that while we are at home in the body we are absent from the Lord. For we walk by faith, not by sight. We are confident, yes, well pleased rather to be absent from the body and to be present with the Lord.

2 Corinthians 5:5–7

"O Death, where is your sting?
O Hades, where is your victory?" The sting of death is sin, and the strength of sin is the law. But thanks be to God, who gives us the victory through our Lord Jesus Christ.

1 Corinthians 15:55–57

For since by man came death, by Man also came the resurrection of the dead. For as in Adam all die, even so in Christ all shall be made alive.

1 Corinthians 15:21–22

Jesus said to her, "I am the resurrection and the life. He who believes in Me, though he may die, he shall live."

John 11:25

Blessed are those who mourn,
For they shall be comforted.

Matthew 5:4

My Journal Page

Date _____

SICKNESS

*"And these signs will follow those
who believe: In My name
they will cast out demons;
they will speak with new tongues;
they will take up serpents;
and if they drink anything deadly,
it will by no means hurt them;
they will lay hands on the sick,
and they will recover."*

—Mark 16:17–18

The Fiery Furnace

Is it just me, or does it seem to you that more and more people are being diagnosed with debilitating or life-threatening illnesses?

In the last year, I've had close friends diagnosed with breast cancer, melanoma, fibromyalgia, prostate cancer, and lymphoma. Some have survived extreme medical treatments and are recovering; some are still battling for their lives; some have been healed. Affected friends struggle to keep their families intact and their lives balanced. They strive to maintain dignity and hope in circumstances that try to rob them of both.

The words *Why, God?* passed my lips more than once, but God didn't reveal any pat answers to me. God's ways are not our ways. His thoughts are not our thoughts. His Word tells us that His plans give us a hope and a future.

King Nebuchadnezzar dictated that everyone in the land

worship a ninety-foot gold statue or be thrown into a blazing furnace. Shadrach, Meshach, and Abed-Nego were young Jewish men who worshiped God and God alone. They would not worship the idol. Furious, the king ordered that the furnace be heated seven times hotter than usual. It was so hot that the raging fire consumed the men who bound them and threw them into the furnace.

Just before being thrown in, Shadrach, Meshach, and Abed-Nego spoke to the king. "O Nebuchadnezzar, we have no need to answer you in this matter. If that is the case, our God whom we serve is able to deliver us from the burning fiery furnace, and He will deliver us from your hand, O king. But if not, let it be known to you, O king, that we do not serve your gods, nor will we worship the gold image which you have set up" (Daniel 3:16–18).

Sometimes we are not able to control our circumstances or our future. We know that this world and its woes are temporary for us. We know that nothing will happen to us that God won't give us grace to walk through. We know that when we are too tired to go on, He will personally carry us with tender strength.

O God, we know that You are able to save us and rescue us. We are asking You to heal us for Your glory. But even if You don't, we will serve You and You alone. As we walk through this fire, conform us to You. Strengthen our bodies and our spirits and stay close to us in the darkness.

For Times of Sickness

Is anyone among you sick? Let him call for the elders of the church, and let them pray over him, anointing him with oil in the name of the Lord. And the prayer of faith will save the sick, and the Lord will raise him up. And if he has committed sins, he will be forgiven.

JAMES 5:14–15

If you diligently heed the voice of the LORD your God and do what is right in His sight, give ear to His commandments and keep all His statutes, I will put none of the diseases on you which I have brought on the Egyptians. For I am the LORD who heals you.

EXODUS 15:26

Surely He shall deliver you from the snare
   of the fowler
And from the perilous pestilence. . . .
You shall not be afraid of the terror by night,
Nor of the arrow that flies by day,
Nor of the pestilence that walks in darkness,
Nor of the destruction that lays waste
   at noonday. . . .

No evil shall befall you,
Nor shall any plague come near your dwelling.

Psalm 91:3, 5-6, 10

So you shall serve the Lord your God, and He will bless your bread and your water. And I will take sickness away from the midst of you.

Exodus 23:25

The Lord will strengthen him on his bed of illness; You will sustain him on his sickbed.

Psalm 41:3

Behold, I will bring it health and healing; I will heal them and reveal to them the abundance of peace and truth.

Jeremiah 33:6

But He was wounded for our transgressions,
He was bruised for our iniquities;
The chastisement for our peace was upon Him,
And by His stripes we are healed.

Isaiah 53:5

Beloved, I pray that you may prosper in all things and be in health, just as your soul prospers.

3 John 2

He sent His word and healed them,
And delivered them from their destructions.

PSALM 107:20

Then Jesus went about all the cities and villages,
teaching in their synagogues, preaching the gospel of
the kingdom, and healing every sickness and every
disease among the people.

MATTHEW 9:35

O LORD my God, I cried out to You,
And You healed me.

PSALM 30:2

Heal me, O LORD, and I shall be healed;
Save me, and I shall be saved,
For You are my praise.

JEREMIAH 17:14

And the whole multitude sought to touch Him,
for power went out from Him and healed them all.

LUKE 6:19

Come, and let us return to the LORD;
For He has torn, but He will heal us;
He has stricken, but He will bind us up.

HOSEA 6:1

My son, give attention to my words;
Incline your ear to my sayings.
Do not let them depart from your eyes;
Keep them in the midst of your heart;
For they are life to those who find them,
And health to all their flesh.

PROVERBS 4:20–22

My Journal Page

Date _____

_____

_____

_____

_____

_____

_____

_____

_____

_____

_____

_____

_____

_____

_____

_____

Anger

"But may the God of all grace, who called us to His eternal glory by Christ Jesus, after you have suffered a while, perfect, establish, strengthen, and settle you."
—1 Peter 5:10

"Be still, and know that I am God."
—Psalm 46:10

Trust His Heart

❦

$\mathscr{D}$ealing with death is not easy for any of us. Whether death is sudden and unexpected or whether it is the culmination of a long illness, we all struggle with letting go of our loved ones. In 1986 four tragic deaths tested my faith and alienated me from the Lord.

My cousin, Ray, was a fun-loving young guy in his twenties. He and his wife, Debbie, had a little boy who was nine months old. Ray was driving home from work in the wee hours of the morning. As he descended a hill, the entire electrical system on his car went out. A giant truck crested the hill behind him, but its driver never saw Ray's car until it was too late. Ray was killed instantly. He left a young wife, a baby, and no life insurance.

Andy Boggs, at twenty-one years old, was an extremely gifted musician and composer who was being treated at Mayo Clinic for a rare type of brain cancer. Andy seemed to respond remarkably well to the treatment, and despite the low survival rate of this cancer, doctors were hopeful. I invited Andy to be a guest on my radio program, and my producer and I both felt an immediate rapport with this brave young man and his family.

Early that year, he went to Mayo for a routine checkup. The doctors were shocked to discover the cancer had spread like wildfire. His parents were told to take him home and make him as comfortable as possible. Andy Boggs died with the promise of musical greatness still in him.

Ron Jones owned a hair and makeup salon in Chicago and was my personal friend. When we met in 1972 he helped me prepare for each level of the Miss America Pageant. We stayed in touch regularly over the years. Ron was a kind man who gave generously to others without thought of cost. When he was diagnosed with brain tumors, I was stunned and filled with dread. I watched those tumors destroy him a little bit at a time. It was a slow, terrible way to die. Ron's family helped him do that with dignity.

Linda Joerres, a mother of four in her thirties, and her husband, Tom, were friends of ours for a number of years. She was diagnosed with cancer that, because of medical error, had already spread to her liver. She endured chemotherapy, radiation, and unbelievable pain at the same time she was sending her youngest off to preschool for the first time.

She wasn't doing well, and I called her husband to see if she was open to visitors. I had such a burden to pray for her. He called back to say that Wednesday would be good. On Wednesday morning my husband called from his office and said, "I think you'd better sit down. Linda Joerres died this morning." I hung up the phone without speaking.

I was so angry with God. I couldn't pray. I couldn't read the Bible. I did not want any pat answers or easy Scriptures. Unresolved pain burned inside me. Then one day in my car I could no longer stop my tears or questions. "Why, God? Why? Why? Why?" Alone in my car, in the quiet of my heart, came a response so clear it seemed almost audible. *I am sovereign.* Silence.

I knew what God was saying. Either He is God or He isn't. If He is, I needed to trust His will in all things—and not just in the things I understood or agreed with. If I was willing to let go of my hurt and my anger and offer it all to Him, in return He would give me His peace and comfort.

Letting go, relinquishing, releasing—giving it all to Him. It's a day-by-day, moment-by-moment challenge. It is never easy to do this, but when we do, it always leads us straight to the heart of God. This chorus tells it all:

> God is too wise to be mistaken.
> God is too good to be unkind.
> So when you don't understand,
> When you don't see His plan,
> When you can't trace His hand,
> Trust His heart.

Lord, in the dark and unexplainable places, teach me to trust Your heart. Thank You for loving me and staying close even when I'm angry and resentful. Teach me the fine art of being still and fill me with the knowledge of Your sovereignty.

For Times of Anger

"Be angry, and do not sin": do not let the sun go down on your wrath.

EPHESIANS 4:26

He who is slow to wrath has great understanding, But he who is impulsive exalts folly.

PROVERBS 14:29

But now you yourselves are to put off all these: anger, wrath, malice, blasphemy, filthy language out of your mouth.

COLOSSIANS 3:8

But I say to you that whoever is angry with his brother without a cause shall be in danger of the judgment. And whoever says to his brother, "Raca!" shall be in danger of the council. But whoever says, "You fool!" shall be in danger of hell fire. Therefore if you bring your gift to the altar, and there remember that your brother has something against you, leave your gift there before the altar, and go your way. First be reconciled to your brother, and then come and offer your gift.

MATTHEW 5:22–24

Beloved, do not avenge yourselves, but rather give place to wrath; for it is written, "Vengeance is Mine, I will repay," says the Lord. Therefore
"If your enemy is hungry, feed him;
If he is thirsty, give him a drink;
For in so doing you will heap coals of fire
    on his head."
Do not be overcome by evil, but overcome evil with good.

ROMANS 12:19–21

Let all bitterness, wrath, anger, clamor, and evil speaking be put away from you, with all malice. And be kind to one another, tenderhearted, forgiving one another, even as God in Christ forgave you.

EPHESIANS 4:31–32

For as the churning of milk produces butter,
And wringing the nose produces blood,
So the forcing of wrath produces strife.

PROVERBS 30:33

So then, my beloved brethren, let every man be swift to hear, slow to speak, slow to wrath; for the wrath of man does not produce the righteousness of God.

JAMES 1:19–20

A soft answer turns away wrath,
But a harsh word stirs up anger. . . .
A wrathful man stirs up strife,
But he who is slow to anger allays contention.

PROVERBS 15:1, 18

*F*or if you forgive men their trespasses, your heavenly Father will also forgive you.

MATTHEW 6:14

*H*e who is slow to anger is better than the mighty,
And he who rules his spirit than he who takes a city.

PROVERBS 16:32

*F*or we know Him who said, "Vengeance is Mine, I will repay," says the Lord. And again, "The LORD will judge His people."

HEBREWS 10:30

A fool's wrath is known at once,
But a prudent man covers shame.

PROVERBS 12:16

Cease from anger, and forsake wrath;
Do not fret—it only causes harm.

PSALM 37:8

A wise man fears and departs from evil,
But a fool rages and is self-confident.
A quick-tempered man acts foolishly,
And a man of wicked intentions is hated.

PROVERBS 14:16–17

An angry man stirs up strife,
And a furious man abounds in transgression.

PROVERBS 29:22

Do not hasten in your spirit to be angry,
For anger rests in the bosom of fools.

ECCLESIASTES 7:9

Fathers, do not provoke your children, lest they
become discouraged.

COLOSSIANS 3:21

The discretion of a man makes him slow to anger,
And his glory is to overlook a transgression.

PROVERBS 19:11

A haughty look, a proud heart,
And the plowing of the wicked are sin

*S*coffers set a city aflame,
But wise men turn away wrath.

My Journal Page

Date _____

FEAR

"For God has not given us a spirit of fear, but of power and of love and of a sound mind."

—2 Timothy 1:7

A Gift for All Seasons

Have you ever had one of those dreams where someone or something is chasing you, and no matter how fast you run your pursuer keeps getting closer and closer until you're nearly overtaken? And then you wake up in a sweat, gasping for breath? Well, several years ago that's how our financial troubles felt.

In the midst of this, Andy suddenly showed up at home in the middle of the day. He sighed deeply and dropped his keys on the island counter in the kitchen. I turned from the sink and saw a husband I hardly recognized. He was ashen, and his shoulders were bent in defeat.

"What's wrong?" I asked.

With tears in his eyes he blurted out, "I'm so afraid that if we lose this house, I'm going to lose you!"

"Andy," I assured him, "I didn't marry this house, I married you."

Nothing can incapacitate us like fear. Fear can paralyze us. Fear can render us incapable of seeing anything but our problems. We lose confidence in who we are. More significantly, we lose awareness of God. In moments of fear, some people compromise their most deeply held principles. Some people roll up into balls of dysfunction and addiction. Some people even take their own lives.

The enemy knows right where to hit us, doesn't he? He wangles his way in, unnoticed at first, and patiently waits for a vulnerable spot to open. Zap. Those fiery arrows start flying. If we are not spending time in the Word and in prayer, and if we do not surround ourselves with loving, encouraging believers, we make ourselves highly susceptible to the wiles of Satan.

The Lord knew we would be highly vulnerable, and so He gave us all an incredible gift—a gift that keeps on giving if we keep on receiving. The gift is the Holy Spirit. Jesus said

He would send Him and that when He came He would guide us in all truth. "For God has not given us a spirit of fear, but of power and of love and of a sound mind" (2 Timothy 1:7).

The disciples who lived and walked and talked with Jesus were incapacitated by fear until the Holy Spirit came upon them. The Bible says that after Jesus died, the disciples were hiding behind locked doors in fear for their lives. Though they knew that the tomb was empty and that Mary Magdalene had seen Jesus, they had not yet seen Him themselves. Suddenly, He was there in the midst of them; a week later He appeared again, and they were still behind locked doors.

Before He ascended He told them not to leave Jerusalem but to wait for the "Promise of the Father" (Acts 1:4). He said, "You shall be baptized with the Holy Spirit not many days from now. . . . You shall receive power when the Holy Spirit has come upon you; and you shall be witnesses to Me in Jerusalem, and in all Judea and Samaria, and to the end of the earth" (Acts 1:5, 8).

These men were terrified, but when God's Spirit anointed them they were bold to proclaim God's Word. Just as the disciples needed the Holy Spirit, so do we. "Now when the apostles who were at Jerusalem heard that Samaria had received the word of God, they sent Peter and John to them, who, when they had come down, prayed for them that they might receive the Holy Spirit. For as yet He had fallen upon none of them. They had only been baptized in the name of the Lord Jesus. Then they laid hands on them, and they received the Holy Spirit" (Acts 8:14–17).

The apostles knew that the new believers needed the Holy Spirit. That same power and boldness are available to every believer today. When someone gives us a gift, our role is to receive it. Today, if there is any fear in your life, exchange it for the living Spirit of God.

Lord, when fear rises up in me it blinds me to who You are. Suddenly the obstacles in my life seem like giants. I ask You right now to fill me with the power, the boldness, and the strength of Your mighty Holy Spirit. I exchange this anxiety and fear for Your awesome gift. Come, Holy Spirit, and fill my entire being with Your presence. I bind the spirit of fear in the name of Jesus and command it to leave. Spirit of the living God, fall fresh on me.

For Times of Fear

Peace I leave with you, My peace I give to you; not as the world gives do I give to you. Let not your heart be troubled, neither let it be afraid.

John 14:27

No evil shall befall you,
Nor shall any plague come near your dwelling;
For He shall give His angels charge over you,
To keep you in all your ways.

Psalm 91:10–11

For God has not given us a spirit of fear, but of power and of love and of a sound mind.

2 Timothy 1:7

There is no fear in love; but perfect love casts out fear, because fear involves torment. But he who fears has not been made perfect in love.

1 John 4:18

Yea, though I walk through the valley of the
    shadow of death,
I will fear no evil;
For You are with me;

Your rod and Your staff, they comfort me.
You prepare a table before me in the presence of
    my enemies;
You anoint my head with oil;
My cup runs over.

Psalm 23:4–5

For you did not receive the spirit of bondage again to fear, but you received the Spirit of adoption by whom we cry out, "Abba, Father."

Romans 8:15

So we may boldly say:
"The Lord is my helper;
I will not fear.
What can man do to me?"

Hebrews 13:6

He who dwells in the secret place of the
    Most High
Shall abide under the shadow of the Almighty. . . .
He shall cover you with His feathers,
And under His wings you shall take refuge;
His truth shall be your shield and buckler.
You shall not be afraid of the terror by night,

Nor of the arrow that flies by day,
Nor of the pestilence that walks in darkness,
Nor of the destruction that lays waste at noonday.
A thousand may fall at your side,
And ten thousand at your right hand;
But it shall not come near you.

PSALM 91:1, 4–7

In righteousness you shall be established;
You shall be far from oppression, for you shall
   not fear;
And from terror, for it shall not come near you.

ISAIAH 54:14

When you pass through the waters, I will be
   with you;
And through the rivers, they shall not overflow you.
When you walk through the fire, you shall not
   be burned,
Nor shall the flame scorch you.

ISAIAH 43:2

God is our refuge and strength,
A very present help in trouble.

PSALM 46:1

*N*o evil shall befall you,
Nor shall any plague come near your dwelling.

PSALM 91:10

*T*he fear of man brings a snare,
But whoever trusts in the LORD shall be safe.

PROVERBS 29:25

*O*h, how great is Your goodness,
Which You have laid up for those who fear You,
Which You have prepared for those who trust
   in You
In the presence of the sons of men!
You shall hide them in the secret place of
   Your presence
From the plots of man;
You shall keep them secretly in a pavilion
From the strife of tongues.

PSALM 31:19–20

*Y*ou are my hiding place;
You shall preserve me from trouble;
You shall surround me with songs of deliverance.
Selah

PSALM 32:7

The LORD is my light and my salvation;
Whom shall I fear?
The LORD is the strength of my life;
Of whom shall I be afraid?

PSALM 27:1

"No weapon formed against you shall prosper,
And every tongue which rises against you
    in judgment
You shall condemn.
This is the heritage of the servants of the LORD,
And their righteousness is from Me,"
Says the LORD.

ISAIAH 54:17

I, even I, am He who comforts you.
Who are you that you should be afraid
Of a man who will die,
And of the son of a man who will be made
    like grass?
And you forget the LORD your Maker,
Who stretched out the heavens
And laid the foundations of the earth;
You have feared continually every day
Because of the fury of the oppressor,

When he has prepared to destroy.
And where is the fury of the oppressor?

ISAIAH 51:12–13

$\mathscr{D}$o not be afraid of sudden terror,
Nor of trouble from the wicked when it comes;
For the LORD will be your confidence,
And will keep your foot from being caught.

PROVERBS 3:25–26

My Journal Page

Date _____

_____

_____

_____

_____

_____

_____

_____

_____

_____

_____

_____

_____

_____

_____

_____

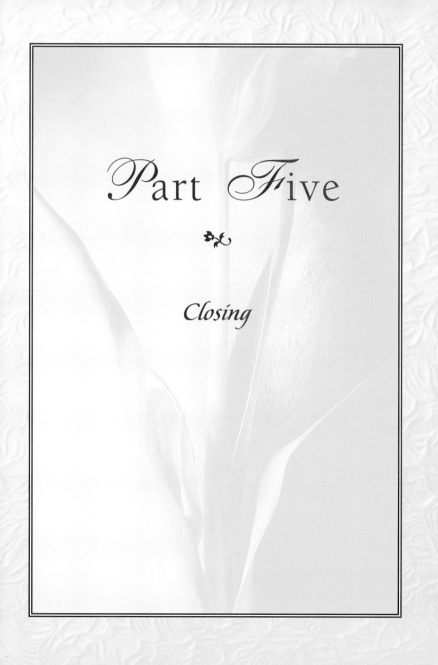

Part Five

Closing

HOLINESS

"Pursue peace with all people,

and holiness, without which

no one will see the Lord."

—Hebrews 12:14

Consecrated to Him

❧

$\mathscr{M}$ost of us would be moderately uncomfortable with the thought that we could be holy. Holiness seems to be an attribute reserved for God, but beyond that a lot of us would have a difficult time trying to verbalize exactly what it is. Yet way back in the book of Leviticus, God clearly says to His people, "Be holy, for I am the LORD your God" (20:7).

It is almost impossible for me to comprehend God's Holiness. His holiness is the antithesis of what I am and what I know, and it evokes all kinds of feelings in me—from sheer terror to trembling reverence. I have been reading numerous Scripture passages and books on the holiness of God, and my reading has caused me to reflect on how cavalierly we treat God in the midst of such incredible blessings. As I was running an errand yesterday, I looked at the scenes passing by my car window. Beautiful homes with lovely yards; people golfing in designer clothing on perfectly manicured fairways; stores stocked with everything we could desire; lakes and trees and wildlife; people fishing and swimming and biking. In the midst of it all, I was struck with how much we are given and how much we take for granted. I was overwhelmed with how much God has provided for us. And I was overwhelmed with how seldom we acknowledge Him for it.

This biblical warning came to mind: "Beware that you do not forget the LORD your God . . . lest—when you have eaten and are full, and have built beautiful houses and dwell in them; and when your herds and your flocks multiply, and your silver and your gold are multiplied, and all that you have is multiplied; when your heart is lifted up, and you forget the LORD your God" (Deuteronomy 8:11–14). Words we need to heed.

When we glimpse the greatness of our God, we often want to do something to honor Him. We are like Peter when he saw Jesus in His glory with Moses and Elijah.

He said, "If You wish, let us make here three tabernacles" (Matthew 17:4).

But in the book of Micah, God tells us what He requires of us to be pleasing to Him. "With what shall I come before the LORD, /And bow myself before the High God? /Shall I come before Him with burnt offerings, /With calves a year old? /Will the LORD be pleased with thousands of rams, /Ten thousand rivers of oil? /Shall I give my firstborn for my transgression, /The fruit of my body for the sin of my soul? /He has shown you, O man, what is good; /And what does the LORD require of you /But to do justly, /To love mercy, /And to walk humbly with your God?" (6:6–8).

God isn't looking for perfect men and women; God isn't asking us to build great monuments to Him. God is looking for people who will reverence Him in their hearts and in their lifestyles. God is looking for people in whom He can take up residence, with whom He can speak and walk, through whom He can work. He is looking for people who are willing to be set apart.

❧

Lord, I know that You understand my shortcomings, for You created me. But I also know that You are holy and awesome and that Your purposes for Your people far exceed what I could dream or imagine. Forgive me for being distracted from You. I bow my heart and my knee to You, the King of kings and Lord of lords. Perform a work in me that I might be pleasing in Your sight, O God. My heart cries out with Your angels as they call to one another, "Holy, Holy, Holy is the LORD of hosts; / The whole earth is full of His glory!" (Isaiah 6:3).

In Holiness

Blessed are the pure in heart,
For they shall see God.

MATTHEW 5:8

To the pure all things are pure, but to those who
are defiled and unbelieving nothing is pure; but even
their mind and conscience are defiled.

TITUS 1:15

Who may ascend into the hill of the LORD?
Or who may stand in His holy place?
He who has clean hands and a pure heart,
Who has not lifted up his soul to an idol,
Nor sworn deceitfully.

PSALM 24:3–4

Therefore if anyone cleanses himself from the
latter, he will be a vessel for honor, sanctified and
useful for the Master, prepared for every good work.

2 TIMOTHY 2:21

A highway shall be there, and a road,
And it shall be called the Highway of Holiness.

The unclean shall not pass over it,
But it shall be for others.
Whoever walks the road, although a fool,
Shall not go astray.

Isaiah 35:8

Who gave Himself for us, that He might redeem us from every lawless deed and purify for Himself His own special people, zealous for good works.

Titus 2:14

And such were some of you. But you were washed, but you were sanctified, but you were justified in the name of the Lord Jesus and by the Spirit of our God.

1 Corinthians 6:11

And you, who once were alienated and enemies in your mind by wicked works, yet now He has reconciled in the body of His flesh through death, to present you holy, and blameless, and above reproach in His sight.

Colossians 1:21–22

And for their sakes I sanctify Myself, that they also may be sanctified by the truth.

John 17:19

Now may the God of peace Himself sanctify you completely; and may your whole spirit, soul, and body be preserved blameless at the coming of our Lord Jesus Christ.

1 Thessalonians 5:23

But we are bound to give thanks to God always for you, brethren beloved by the Lord, because God from the beginning chose you for salvation through sanctification by the Spirit and belief in the truth.

2 Thessalonians 2:13

Then I will give them one heart, and I will put a new spirit within them, and take the stony heart out of their flesh, and give them a heart of flesh, that they may walk in My statutes and keep My judgments and do them; and they shall be My people, and I will be their God.

Ezekiel 11:19–20

My Journal Page

Date _____

_____

_____

_____

_____

_____

_____

_____

_____

_____

_____

_____

_____

_____

_____

_____

_____

_____

_____

In Closing:
"Stand Firm"

❦

My dear friends, you and I are in an intense battle that has eternal consequences. Whether we recognize it or choose to participate has no bearing on the reality of the battle—but, it certainly has a bearing on the outcome. In Ephesians 6, Paul tells us, "For we do not wrestle against flesh and blood, but against principalities, against powers, against the rulers of the darkness of this age, against spiritual hosts of wickedness in the heavenly places" (v. 12).

In response to this battle, God, Himself, has supplied us with all that we need to persevere and push through to victory. It's called "the whole armor of God, that you may be able to withstand in the evil days" (v. 13).

I know two couples, all dear friends, who would not think of starting their day without consciously stopping and prayerfully putting on the whole armor of God. As I've been engaged in battle in my own life recently, I've determined to do the same. Over and over again in these verses Paul says, "Stand! Stand! Stand!" There are times in the battle when, having done all we know to do, we simply dig in our heels, set our face like a flint, and stand firm until the Lord brings victory.

Therefore put on God's complete armor, *that you may be able to resist and stand your ground on the evil day [of danger], and, having done all [the crisis demands], to stand [firmly in your place]. Stand therefore [hold your ground], having tightened the* belt of truth *around your loins, and having put on the* breastplate of integrity *and of moral rectitude and right standing with God; and having* shod your feet *in preparation [to face the enemy with the firm-footed stability, the promptness and the readiness produced by the good news] of the* Gospel of peace *[Isa. 52:7.] Lift up over all the [covering]* shield of saving faith, *upon which you can quench all the flaming missiles* of the wicked [one]. And take the helmet of salvation *and the* sword the Spirit wields, which is the Word of God. Pray at all times *(on every occasion, in every season) in the Spirit, with all [manner of] prayer and entreaty. To that end keep alert and watch with strong purpose and perseverance, interceding in behalf of all the saints (God's consecrated people). (Ephesians 6:13–18 AMPLIFIED BIBLE)*

Lord, teach me to point my face to the storm, and give me the determination to stand my ground in the midst of the battle until You bring the victory. My hope is in You, my Shield and the Defender of my soul.

Benediction

"Now may the God of peace who brought up our Lord Jesus from the dead, that great Shepherd of the sheep, through the blood of the everlasting covenant, make you complete in every good work to do His will, working in you what is well pleasing in His sight, through Jesus Christ, to whom be glory forever and ever. Amen."

—Hebrews 13:20–21

My Journal Page

Date _____

_____

_____

_____

_____

_____

_____

_____

_____

_____

_____

_____

_____

_____

_____

_____

_____

_____

_____

My Journal Page

Date _____

_____

_____

_____

_____

_____

_____

_____

_____

_____

_____

_____

_____

_____

_____

_____

My Journal Page

Date _____

_____
_____
_____
_____
_____
_____
_____
_____
_____
_____
_____
_____
_____
_____
_____
_____
_____
_____

My Journal Page

Date _____

_____

_____

_____

_____

_____

_____

_____

_____

_____

_____

_____

_____

_____

_____

_____

_____

_____

My Journal Page

Date _____

_____

_____

_____

_____

_____

_____

_____

_____

_____

_____

_____

_____

_____

_____

_____

_____

_____

_____

My Journal Page

Date _____

_____
_____
_____
_____
_____
_____
_____
_____
_____
_____
_____
_____
_____
_____
_____
_____
_____

My Journal Page

Date _____